READING ON THE RUN

CONTINUUM READING CONCEPTS

Dr. J. Robert Clinton

ISBN 1-932814-14-0

Barnabas Publishers
P.O. Box 6006
Altadena, Ca 91003-6006

Printed in the United States of America.

Cover Design & Book Layout by D.M. Battermann

TABLE OF CONTENTS

IV. WRITING A BOOK REVIEW
USING READING CONTINUUM CONCEPTS

The Need For Differing
Levels Of Reading

Introduction

Leaders need to be able to process large amounts of reading materials since the leadership field is so broad and so much requires comparative skills. The ability to read much requires selectivity skills. Continuum Reading Concepts teach reading skills which require purposive reading, comparative skills which build on what is already known, and selectivity skills which screen out material on a need to know basis.

Purpose

Continuum Reading Concepts are useful to direct a reader to process vast amounts of information at some level of acquisition and lesser amounts at more in depth levels of acquisition and evaluation, with an ultimate view of identifying and using concepts in one's own leadership.

Rationale

The reading continuum is based on several assumptions:

1. People who read with a plan in mind for the reading will be more effective readers than those who do not.
2. Not every word has to be read from a book in order to profit from it. In fact, most books do not need to be read in entirety to profit from them.
3. A person having read a book at an assessment reading level (scan, ransack, or browse) is a quantum leap ahead of one who has not read the book at all.
4. Most books do not need to be read at evaluation level (pre-read, read and study) since most books do not have a well integrated theme nor dedicated structure.
5. The amount of literature coming out in the leadership area is well beyond the normal reading (word by word) capacity of most leaders. Hence, skills which allow "learning shortcuts", such as continuum reading skills, will be welcome by most.

6. Most leaders will need psychological release from the need to read every word in a book before they can really feel comfortable with and profit from continuum reading skills.

ACKNOWLEDGEMENT

In my graduate studies at Columbia Bible College, Professor James Hatch introduced me to Mortimer J. Adler's book, **How To Read A Book**. That book introduced me into a framework for approaching higher level in-depth reading skills. It also showed me that I could not afford to do that kind of reading for most books. That forced me to generate the assessment approaches for less in-depth reading.

THE READING CONTINUUM — OVERVIEW

INTRODUCTION

Most people learn to read by reading every word on every page. The reading continuum is based on the assumption that one does not have to read every word in order to benefit from information. One can read different books differently and obtain useful information without having to read every word of every book. The continuum has at the right the most detailed level of reading - called study. At the left is the lightest kind of reading called scan. In between are various kinds of reading each increasing (in terms of depth, intensity, time invested, amount covered) as one moves to the right. Each level to the right includes the various features involved in all reading levels to the left. The ability to read various kinds of books differently is a valuable skill and almost necessity for anyone involved in leadership and leadership training, since so much has been written. (Determine

THE READING CONTINUUM

	Scan	Ransack	Browse	Pre-Read	In Depth Read	Study
Key Ideas	(Overview Contents)	(New Ideas; Specific Ideas)	(Some indepth contextual analysis)	(Determine Thematic Intent; Structural Intent)	(Analysis thematic intent; evaluation analysis)	(Repeated work in book; Comparative analysis)

◄━━ Assesment Levels ━━► ◄━━ Evaluation Levels ━━►

Many Books ◄━━━━━━━━   ━━━━━━━► Fewer books
Should be read   should be read

COMMENT

The reading continuum is not related to *speed reading skills.* Speed reading programs teach one how to rapidly scan words. A person can be a very fast or very slow reader and still use continuum reading concepts. Continuum reading concepts teach one how to pick and choose which words, paragraphs, pages, chapters and sections to be read, and how to read them for information without having to read every word.

NESTED

Each level to the right on the continuum assumes that the book has been previously been read by all the levels to the left (at least superficially) prior to reading at that new level.

FEEDBACK ON READING CONTINUUM OVERVIEW

1. *The techniques described in this booklet pertain to what kind of reading?* (Check any which you feel apply.)
   ___ a. reading for pleasure
   ___ b. reading for information
   ___ c. speed reading
   ___ d. reading to prepare for taking a test on a book

2. *According to the major ideas of the reading continuum* (Check any which you feel apply.)
   ___ a. all books should be read in the same way
   ___ b. not all the material of every book has to be read (word for word) in order for a reader to profit from the reading
   ___ c. relatively speaking, fewer books should be read at evaluation levels (in an in-depth way)
   ___ d. relatively speaking, more books should be read at assessment levels of reading than evaluation levels of reading (at lesser levels of)
   ___ e. all books should not be read in the same way

3. *What do you think might be a hindrance or hindrances to someone learning to read along the continuum?*

ANSWERS ———1. x b; 2. x b. x c. x d. x e; 3. A psychological barrier against learning to read along the continuum is the necessity to feel a book has not been read unless one has threaded one's eyes through every word. The inability to recognize differences in books as to content, importance, structure, integration, presentation of new material, etc.

SCAN READING

INTRODUCTION

Scan reading allows one to survey the potential value of reading a book without having committed too much time to it. It is the initial approach to reading a book.

DEFINITION

Scan reading is an overview approach to the reading of a book. This involves a careful reading of the table of contents, introductory information, "dust cover" remarks, along with any information on the author which will allow at least a cursory understanding of what the book is about and how it is organized with a view toward determining what further level along the continuum the book should be read.

COMMENTS

Scanning also includes "thumbing" through the book to note any conclusions, summary statements, charts, tables, possibility of useful quotes, illustrations, etc.

SIX RESULTS

When you have scanned a book you will:

1. Know who wrote the book,
2. Have identified the author's perspective,
3. Know how the book is organized,
4. Recognize what the author is trying to accomplish,
5. Have identified further assessment reading possibilities (ransacking/browsing),
6. Have made a decision concerning evaluative reading (whether to do: e.g. will do now, will do in future, will not do, decide after ransacking or browsing; which level to do: pre-read, in-depth read or study).

TIME

Scanning a book requires spending enough time to give involved responses to the 6 basic results listed above. Some books could be scanned in as little as 15 minutes. Some books may take as much as 2 hours.

COMMENT

Normally you will not record the results of a scan reading, especially for results 1-3 and for 6 where no further work will be done. However, where you intend to do further work in the book, such as implied as in 5 or 6, or if you intend to review the work or recommend it to others, it is a good idea to record your results.

EXAMPLE OF SCAN READING

INTRODUCTION

Below I have recorded my scan results for the book listed. The time for scanning this book was a little less than an hour.

EXAMPLE 1 OF SCAN READING
Dick Eastman's, **The Hour That Changes The World**

RESULTS

1. Author:

    Dick Eastman is part of a prayer movement that is backed by World Literature Crusade. He holds eight-hour training sessions called "Change The World School Of Prayer."

2. Author's Perspective:

    The author has experienced the power of prayer and has sensed that God is doing something special around the world and is awakening many to pray. As a result, he is part of a movement that is calling many to pray.

3. Organization of Book:

    There is an introduction and 12 major chapters followed by a conclusion and an appendix. Each chapter discusses a major aspect of the prayer hour. The introduction gives the 12 aspect circular model for praying for an hour. Its focus is motivational. Matthew 26:40-41 is used as the Biblical focus for the model. Each of the 12 aspects of praying has a biblical foundation given. Each gives practical suggestions concerning some major aspect of praying such as: praise, waiting, confession, scripture praying, watching, intercession, petition, thanksgiving, singing, meditation, listening, and praise. The conclusion asks for a commitment to prayer.

4. What the Author wants to accomplish:
   The book is organized around the 12 fold circular model. The basic idea is to help believers have a practical method of praying for an hour a day. Each of the 12 focus points involves 5 minutes of praying.

5. Further assessment reading:
   The Bibliography is definitely worth ransacking. The sections entitled *Waiting* and *Scripture Praying* should be ransacked for more ideas. *Watching* and **Meditating** should be browsed.

6. Further Evaluative Reading:
   The book does not require pre-reading, reading or study.

TIME INVOLVED: About 45 minutes

EXAMPLE 2 OF SCAN READING
LEADERS AND LEADERSHIP by Bogardus

INTRODUCTION
Below, I have recorded my scan results for the book listed. The time for scanning this book was a little less than an hour.

RESULTS
1. Author:
   Emory S. Bogardus was a professor at the University of Southern California in the field of sociology. His sociological field of interest was leadership. He wrote this book toward the last quarter of the trait theory era. This book was part of an important series published by Appleton-Century-Crofts, Inc. of New York—The Century Social Science Series. This alone shows his stature. One does not publish in a technical series with a major publisher without being of high status in a field.

2. Author's Perspective:

   The author, both in the title of the book and the preface, indicates that leadership is best determined from actual life-history studies of leaders. He studied hundreds of leaders' biographies and autobiographies and did comparative analysis to arrive at his findings. It is clear that the author has taken the best findings of the Great Man Era and sociological research methodology of the Trait Era and combined them as his approach to generating findings about leadership.

3. Organization of Book:

   There are three major sections to the book: I. An introductory section (called Part I) containing two chapters. This gives his conceptualization on leaders and leadership and points out the background for context for understanding the other two major sections. II. A major section dealing with leaders and the three major factors determining their emergence (called Part II Origins in Heredity, 2 chapters, Part III, Origins in Social Stimuli, 3 chapters, and Part IV, Origins in Personality, 7 chapters). III. A major section dealing with leadership, which identifies principles and theories dealing with different aspects of leadership. This contains 9 chapters, each of which apparently talks about some leadership theory or some area of major leadership principles.

4. What the Author Intends to Accomplish:

   The author is presenting preliminary findings of his comparative research using life-history case studies. His intent is to stimulate further research and discussion concerning his findings and to demonstrate the validity of studying leader's lives to get at leadership.

5. Further Assessment Reading:

   Open Ransack the third section of the book (9 chapters for general leadership principles); Browse Section I to see Bogardus' integrated approach to leadership.

6. Further Evaluative Reading:

   The book does not require pre-reading, reading or study.

OUTLINE SHEET FOR SCAN READING

Name of Person Doing Scan Reading:

Name of Book:

Time Involved:

6 Scan Results

1.   Author:

2.   Author's Perspective:

3.   Organization of Book:

4.   What the Author Intends to Accomplish:

5.   Further Assessment Reading:

6.   Further Evaluative Reading:

FEEDBACK ON SCAN READING

1. To read a book at Scan level requires: (check any which apply)
    __ a. one hour
    __ b. two hours
    __ c. differs with different people
    __ d. differs with each book
    __ e. depends on being able to get answers corresponding to the 6 results

2. From your experience with books, what would you suggest would give help toward answers for result 1?

    Result 1. Know who wrote the book,

3. From your experience with books, what would you suggest would give help toward answers for result 2?

    Result 2. Have identified the author's perspective,

4. From your experience with books, what would you suggest would give help toward answers for result 3?

    Result 3 Know how the book is organized,

5. From your experience with books, what would you suggest would give help toward answers for result 4?

    Result 4. Recognize what the author is trying to accomplish,

6. From your experience with books, what would you suggest would give help toward answers for result 5?

    Result 5. Have identified any ransacking/browsing possibilities,

7. From your experience with books, what would you suggest would give help toward answers for result 6?

Result 6. Have made a decision concerning pre-read, in-depth read, or study (e.g. will do now, will do in future, will not do).

ANSWERS ———

1. x c. x d. x e. (as you become more proficient at scanning your time for scanning will decrease)

2. Usually the publishers have promotional material giving some general information about an author which they place on the "dust cover," i.e. the temporary outside paper jacket on the book (if hard-back) or the back inside cover (if paperback). Libraries usually cut out the author information from the dust cover and paste it to the back inside cover of a book. Sometimes a title page gives information on the author (such as a title, present role, etc.) A foreword or preface often gives information about the author. In looking for this result, you are not just looking for a name but information that will help you under-stand the author's experience and background with the subject matter of the book, what prompted him/her to write, etc.

3. The answers to question 2 above also help out on this result. Further, there may be hints throughout the book itself which give in-formation on this result. There may be personal illustrations, aside comments, or footnotes which help you see the basic perspective from which the author is approaching the subject matter. Much can be learned about the author's perspective from scanning the bibliography (what books included, what excluded, various author's perspectives of those included or avoided). Often, the section and chapter titles will hint at the author's perspective. However, the preface will be the most helpful in determining the author's perspective and intent.

4. Usually the preface and table of contents will give you the most help in seeing the author's organization of material. Occasionally dust cover information will point out the author's organization. Sometimes an introduction will give this information.

5. The preface or table of contents will give the most information concerning what the author is trying to accomplish. Dust covers usu-ally give a promotional perspective regarding author intent.

6. The table of contents (if semantic titles are used rather than cute titles) will give help on this result. Your actual thumb through of the

book will be the most help on this. For a well organized book, the introductory paragraph and summary paragraphs can be scanned rapidly for ransacking and browsing evaluation.

7. The preface information along with your analysis of the table of contents will enable you to recognize whether the book is developing a major theme in an integrated fashion. If the book is developing a major theme in an integrated fashion and is structured to accomplish it (and if there is much new material to you and you don't have a basal book to compare it to) then you should probably decide to read the book at an evaluation level. Your further assessment levels (ransack and browse) will help you confirm your necessity for evaluation level reading. A book that is not integrated should almost always be read only at an assessment level.

Ransack Reading

Introduction
When you are relatively familiar with certain topics you may not need to read every chapter in a book but may choose to read very selectively. That is, you may read given portions to see if they add any new ideas or ideas different than those you are already aware of. *Closed ransacking* refers to reading while only looking for a pre-selected topic of interest. *Open ransacking* refers to reading while looking for new ideas.

Definition
Ransack reading refers to the technique of looking through a book in order to see what it says concerning a specific topic of interest or combing through a book on relatively familiar material to see if it has any new ideas not known to you.

Definition
Closed Ransacking refers to rapid reading to compare or contrast what is said with some already known idea or ideas in mind.

Definition
Open Ransacking refers to rapid reading to see if there is some new idea or new slant on an idea concerning some specific area of interest.

Six Possible Results
When you have ransacked a book you will have:
1. Noted a new idea on a pre-selected topic of interest to you,
2. Noted a contrasting or differing idea on some pre-selected topic of interest to you,
3. Determined that the book has nothing to add to your pre-selected topic of interest,
4. Gained something worth noting which is of interest to you on any topic,
5. Determined that nothing of interest to you can be gained from the book,

6. Made a tentative decision concerning pre-read, in-depth read or study (e.g. will do now, will do in future, not necessary to do, decide after ransacking or browsing).

HINTS

1. Books which deal with material already familiar to you normally should be ransacked. For example, once you have read a book dealing with instructional objectives you can easily ransack other books on the topic; simply look for different ways they define the concept. Look for any new ideas, verbs used, ways of measuring, etc.

2. Books which contain a series of papers or articles done by different authors is a natural for ransacking. Rarely does such a book develop a coherent thesis. Hence, it is not necessary to read everything but simply to pick and choose according to topics of interest. Gerber's book, **Discipling Through Theological Education by Extension** is a natural for ransacking.

3. The more narrowly you pre-select your topic of interest, the more rapidly you can look just for items on that issue.

EXAMPLE OF OPEN RANSACK READING

BOGARDUS', LEADERS AND LEADERSHIP

INTRODUCTION

Below I give the results of an open ransack of Emory S. Bogardus', **Leaders and Leadership**. From the scan reading (see page 8), I had noted that I should ransack the last 9 chapters using the general pre-selected topic of leadership principles. This is an open ransack in that I have a topic that I am looking for but it is a rather broad topic. If I were to say that I was ransacking for a specific principle, say Goodwin's expectation principle, then it would be closed ransacking. Closed ransacking, looking for a very specific topic, allows for a rapid read through. Open ransacking, like browsing, requires more careful detailed reading and hence takes a little more time than closed ransacking. I'll fill out the standard outline sheet so you will have it as a model.

Outline Sheet for Ransack Reading

Name of Person Doing Ransack Reading: Bobby Clinton
Name of Book: **Leaders and Leadership** by Emory S. Bogardus
___ Closed Ransacking - Specific idea being ransacked
_x_ Open Ransacking - General topic being ransacked: statements or illustrations of leadership principles
Time Involved: 1 and 1/2 hours

Six Possible Ransack Results

1. New ideas on the pre-selected idea or topic:

Ch. XVII Focalization of Psychic Energy The "focalization of psychic energy" theory of leadership means that a person of normal mental and physical ability may, by deliberate concentration of his energy, attain to superior levels of achievement and hence become a leader, page 218 Kinds of focalization: use of spare moments (Andrew Carnegie example); page 220 partial life focalization (football player for a short season); page 221 whole life focalization, "Early in life a person may dedicate himself wholeheartedly and completely to certain basic principles. All phases of his life are devoted to one major aim. Nothing sidetracks." (example of Benjamin Franklin's devotion to industry and thrift) page 222; Willie Hoppe 2nd Ball principle, Doing today's work in such a way that tomorrow's or next week's or next month's, etc. will be easy, page 223, 224. Comment: "Life focalization often revolves about an idea. It resolves to put this into as universal operation as possible," page 225. See also Andrew Carnegie's advice to young men: "Make yourself master in some one line," page 225.

Ch. XVIII Flashes of Insight - "Flashes of insight are transitory, if not captured on the spot... To conserve flashes of insight is basic to leadership," page 235.

Ch. XIX Ability In Disability - In Alfred Adler's theories, inferiority and compensation, there lies the basis for an interesting principle of leadership. Compensation or over-compensation for defects and failures can make a person a strong leader in those particular areas.

EXAMPLE OF OPEN RANSACK READING
BOGARDUS', LEADERS AND LEADERSHIP cont.

1. New ideas on the pre-selected idea or topic-continued:
   Ch. XX Balance and Integration - suggested that there is often a need for opposite trait pairs to make a good leader. Some opposite trait pairs listed for: aggressiveness and inhibition; spontaneity and standardization; vision and concentration; optimism and pessimism. Ch. XXI
   Polarization and Saturation - concept of reaching maximum potential and trying to go beyond: "The law of diminishing returns of leadership... A person may reach a point of leadership beyond which his activity begins to decline in value," page 264.
   Ch. XXIII Achievement and Appreciation - "Appreciating is a quality of followership," page 285.
2. Contrasting or differing idea on pre-selected idea or topic: did not see any.
3. Nothing New of Note On Pre-Selected Topic or Idea.
   Check here ____
4. Saw something of interest on Other than selected Idea or Topic:
   Ch. XVIII Flashes of Insight - Ordinary learners in any field progress by flashes of insight, page 231. Related to learning theory.
5. Nothing New Can Be Gained From This Book.
   Check here ____
6. Decision For Further Reading

   _x_ should read at browse level: Read Chapters 1 and 2 to get Bogardus' understanding of basic definitions about leaders and leadership.
   ____ should read at pre-read level
   ____ should read at in-depth level
   ____ should read at study level
   ____ no further reading needed

EXAMPLE OF CLOSED RANSACK READING

HENDRICKS' TEACHING TO CHANGE LIVES

NAME OF PERSON DOING RANSACK READING: Bobby Clinton

NAME OF BOOK: Howard Hendricks' book, **Teaching To Change Lives**
- Develop a Passion for Communicating God's Words to Adults or
Children - in the Church, in the Home, in Bible Study Groups, or in
School.

CLOSED RANSACKING - specific idea being ransacked: Ransack Chapter
1, The Law of the Teacher, as it pertains to Illustrations of Mentoring,
or teaching principles which relate to the 6 mentor characteristics or
the 8 ways mentors help proteges. I am looking for mentoring ideas
which fit with a teacher's role.

TIME INVOLVED: About 35 minutes

SIX POSSIBLE RANSACK RESULTS
(1, 2, and 6 apply to this ransack)

1. New Ideas or other helpful information on the pre-selected idea or
topic:

Characteristic 1, can readily see potential in a person: see Walt
illustration, page 8, which radically turned Howard Hendricks around
as a boy. This also illustrates function 4, modeling and using Goodwin's
Expectation Principle. Characteristic 4, is patience, recognizing that it
takes time and experience for a person to develop. See illustration of
elderly female teacher from a town in Michigan's Upper Peninsula, (84
of the boys who sat under her year by year are now in full-time voca-
tional Christian ministry - 22 are graduates of Dallas Theological Semi-
nary). Function 1, giving timely advice which encourages the protege:
father's advice on page 26. Under the general Law of the Teacher and
sub-principle of Maintaining a learning posture (a consistent study pro-
gram and a consistent approach to learning from people) Hendricks
has some good information. On page 26 Hendricks notes how important it is to learn from daily experiences from people. He points out

that books and people are probably the most important factors in your development.

Further on that same page, Hendricks points out how his father taught him to listen. Basically the advice showed something we all know. So we need to listen more and talk less especially around someone who is supposed to know something, that is, have expertise in some area. From this, I derive the Law of the Protege. PROTEGES LEARN TO LISTEN AND LEARN ALL THEY CAN FROM MENTORS.

Under the general Law of the Teacher and sub-principle of Getting to Know your students, Hendricks (on page 27, 28) gives an illustration which is most likely a key to characteristic 1. He describes a teacher who became quite successful with junior high boys. When Hendricks probed the teacher to find out the secret of his success, he found that the teacher very seriously prayed for each of the boys in his class. In order to specifically pray for the boys in terms of their real needs and current situations, he had to learn about their personal lives. What he learned and what he prayed made him a teacher whose teaching was relevant and challenging to his students. Note the application of the Samuel Ministry Prayer Principle. Mentors who operate in a teacher role will increase their effectiveness many fold if they apply this principle. Characteristic 4 being reinforced, can tolerate mistakes, brashness, abrasiveness, etc. in a person in order to see potential develop. On page 29, I noted that Hendricks frequently asks teachers to identify kids in a class whom the teacher likes the most. The obvious implications were that kids who are not liked often demonstrate characteristics that may be unpleasing to the teacher but which turn out to be early indicators of leadership potential - if the kid can be reached and turned on instead of turned off.

2. Contrasting or differing idea on pre-selected idea or topic: Negative example of Goodwin's expectation principle, page 28. Hendricks gave a personal example of a teacher in the fifth grade who expected him to be a bad boy. He lived up to those expectations. This points out the importance of challenging potential leaders toward positive growth.

6. Decision For Further Reading

   _x_   should read at browse level:

Outline Sheet for Ransack Reading

Name of Person Doing Ransack Reading:

Name of Book:

____ Closed Ransacking - specific idea being ransacked:

____ Open Ransacking - general topic being ransacked:

Time Involved:

6 Possible Ransack Results

1. New ideas or other helpful information on the pre-selected idea or topic:

2. Contrasting or differing idea on pre-selected idea or topic:

3. Nothing New of Note On Pre-Selected Topic or Idea
          Check here ____

4. Saw something of interest on Other than selected Idea or Topic

5. Nothing New Can Be Gained For This Book
          Check here ____

6. Decision For Further Reading
          ____ should read at browse level:
          ____ should read at pre-read level
          ____ should read at in-depth read level
          ____ should read at study level
          ____ no further reading needed

FEEDBACK ON RANSACK READING

1. Which of the following would not be a good candidate for ransack reading?

    ____ a.   a text on material, all of which is new to you

    ____ b.   a collection of essays from different authors on some general area familiar to you

    ____ c.   a well integrated book dealing with familiar material

    ____ d.   none of the above

2. Suppose you had determined from your scan reading that a book is not an integrated book but is dealing basically with new material. Most likely you should

    ____ a.   decide not to do further continuum reading

    ____ b.   ransack the book noting all the new ideas.

    ____ c.   browse the book

    ____ d.   none of the above

3. What is the underlying rationale of ransacking a book? (Check any which apply)

    ____ a.   a rapid reading of a book with an objective in mind allows for more productive processing of information

    ____ b.   a rapid reading of a book containing much familiar material does not require reading all of the book, just the portions which deal with new or different material than is already known

    ____ c.   a book containing material not known to the reader must be read at evaluation levels.

    ____ d.   Comparison or contrast of information presented with what is already familiar and well-known allows for affirmation of the known or going for the known to the unknown where new ideas or new slants are introduced. These are both important learning methodologies.

Answers ————

1. <u>x</u> a; 2. <u>x</u> c; You can't really ransack brand new material for ransacking requires comparison of what is presented with something already known. The book is not integrated so is not worthy of evaluation level reading. Therefore, browsing is the only thing left on the continuum reading to do. 3. <u>x</u> a, <u>x</u> b, <u>x</u> d.

Browse Reading

Introduction

Having scanned a book you may decide that you are relatively familiar with the material and want to explore in some detail a given topic of interest. You will read a book in this way when you decide that the author is saying something of real interest to you and you want a detailed and thorough understanding of what the author is saying. Detailed reading of an extended portion of a book is what is meant by browsing. A section of a chapter or an entire chapter on a special topic of interest would be the object of browsing. Often you will discover browsing material when ransacking for a new idea. Browsing is a must with unfamiliar material since you can't compare it.

Definition

Browsing is dipping into certain portions of a book to study in detail some discussion of a topic in its contextual treatment.

Three Results

1. Answer evaluation type questions on the limited portion of the book which you read such as:

- what did the author say?
- how well did he/she say it?
- what did he/she leave unsaid?
- how does this book compare with something else?
- how useful is it?

2. Place the limited portion being browsed in the total context of the book so as not to misperceive the author's intent.

3. Decide whether or not your interpretation of the limited portion will require you to pre-read or in-depth read the book for thematic content or structural intent.

Comment

The browsing technique can be used with any size contextual unit. The two-fold approach involved in the concept is the same. Identifying concisely the actual contextual flow of the unit (usually requires word by word reading) and seeing the fit of the unit in the next larger size contextual unit - usually requires scan plus browse techniques. Sizes of units that I browse include:

- paragraphs (especially chapter introductions and summary or conclusion paragraphs),
- chapter sections (a consecutive group of paragraphs relating to a major idea of a chapter),
- whole chapters,
- parts of a section of a book (several chapters developing some single aspect of a major idea of a section of a book),
- sections of a book (entire groups of chapters developing a major idea of the thesis of the book),
- the whole book.

COMMENT
Frequently, I will browse the preface and introduction of a book then browse the conclusion of it and do whatever other browsing or ransacking needed to fit the conclusion into the overall context of the book.

EXAMPLE OF BROWSE READING

DOOHAN'S, LEADERSHIP IN PAUL
Name of Person Doing Browse Reading: Bobby Clinton
Name of Book: Helen Doohan's , **Leadership in Paul**

Unit Being Browsed:
____ 1. paragraphs: identify larger units,
____ 2. chapter sections (a consecutive group of paragraphs relating to a major idea of a chapter): identify extent of chapter section,
_x_ 3. whole chapters: identify which ones: Conclusion chapter,
____ 4. parts of a section of a book (several chapters developing some single aspect of a major idea of a section of a book): Identify extent of the parts of the section,

_x_ 5. sections of a book (entire groups of chapters developing a
major idea of the thesis of the book). Identify extent of the
section. The final chapter of the book is an entire section
dealing with conclusions of the whole book,
___ 6. the whole book.

Time Involved: about 1 hour for the browse (previous scan time of
1 and 1/2 to 2 hours)

PRELIMINARY EXPLANATION:

There are three major sections of the book:

Section I.

Theoretical Leadership Concepts Used as Standards in the Book

Section II.

Analysis of 4 Major Pauline Leadership Situations

Section III.

Conclusion as to Findings on Pauline Leadership

The chapter I am browsing is Section III.

In beginning to browse the Conclusion section in the first paragraph one sentence used the phrase "essential qualities of religious leadership." Since it was obvious that her conclusions would use this, I was
forced to ransack the introductory chapter to understand the concepts
behind the phrase. I ransacked that chapter and noted her theoretical
basis for assessing leadership. She combines a thorough study of secular
leadership theory with her own study of Old Testament (4 major ideas
noted) and New Testament Religious leadership (10 major ideas). From
this synthesis of ideas, she summarizes religious leadership in terms of
two dynamic concepts and about 6 implications (i.e. manifestations).
With this ransacking effort, I was ready to proceed with the browse of
the concluding chapter. See especially page 22 for Old Testament characteristics of religious leadership , pages 22 and 23 for New Testament
characteristics of religious leadership, and pages 23 and 24 for the summary results of the essentials of religious leadership into two dynamic
concepts along with 6 implications.

One further note: Doohan writes frequently with brevity, terse sentences, and sentences that are pregnant with all kinds of implications. Her sentences often require heavy reflection and understanding of lots of background information both of the Bible and leadership theory. I have the same background in terms of leadership theory as she does having studied almost all of the authors she draws from. My biblical outside reading is not as extensive as hers but my actual biblical knowledge is on par with hers so that I can in fact work on her sentences and arrive at very important insights.

Doohan's analysis of Paul's leadership development is purely in terms of the leadership functions being performed, rather than his development in personal character or ministerial skills which is done here at the School of World Mission in our leadership development theory approach. In the School of World Mission, the focus is on the personal development of the leader.

1. Note any observations of ideas, relevant insights, illustrations, biblical exegesis, quotes or other information useful to you. Where important, you may wish to identify the unit being browsed along with the relevant information.

I can summarize her conclusions in the following statements using my own wording.

The longitudinal (diachronic) study of Pauline leadership following a chronological ordering of his epistles show that Paul developed as a leader - she particularly noted development in leadership style, (page 161, 162).

Doohan gives succinct summaries of her findings of each of the major epistles she analyzed. As I read each of those succinct summaries, I was forced to ransack back to the chapters where necessary. For each of those epistles she used a fourfold structural approach: explanation of leadership situation, the delineation of the major issues and their implications, the analysis of the leadership act itself involving interaction and response between leader, followers and the dynamics of the situation.

In the Thessalonian letter, Doohan attributes Paul's success to confidence, relationships with the Thessalonian church, and an approach which fit the situation he was dealing with. The full details and analysis of this particular leadership act is given in chapter 1, Early Leadership in Paul: The First Letter to the Thessalonians.

In the Galatian letter, Doohan shows Paul as a fallible leader who must confront a situation. Identification of issues and implications of those issues along with the strong assertive confrontation are part of the leadership style seen there. Chapter 2, Conflict and Confrontation: The Letter to the Galatians covers her in-depth analysis of this extended series of leadership acts.

In the Corinthian leadership situation (a series of leadership acts over several years) there were specific issues identified, and a recognition that the situation changed over the several years involved in the series of leadership acts. She notes that he uses persuasion, modeling, argument, and judgement along with appeal to his authority. She notes also that he reacts somewhat defensively at times in the midst of highly emotional controversy. Chapter 3, Division, Diversity, Defense: 1 and 2 Corinthians covers her detailed analysis.

In the Roman letter, Doohan sees Paul emerging as a mature leader who can correctly identify the critical issue facing leadership in the Roman situation. She describes Paul's efforts as integrative, raising of awareness of theological consciousness, clarifying of issues and implications and laying of groundwork for future leadership influence. Chapter 4, Maturity and Refinement: The Letter to the Romans contains the in-depth analysis.

In her analysis of the Philippian situation, Doohan sees Paul as a very mature leader who prepares his followers for a future in which he will not be a part. He affirms future leadership and delegates responsibility to them. He is modeling leadership transition which seeks to insure the ongoing success of the church. Chapter 5, A Final Perspective: The Letter to the Philippians describes her detailed analysis.

Doohan assesses Pauline leadership as genuine religious leadership according to the standards lined out in chapter 1.

1. His leadership begins with a unique call, (destiny preparation).
2. His apostolic mission flows out of his experience and on-going destiny experiences with God (destiny revelation/destiny confirmation).
3. His authority is established repeatedly by the Lord Himself as

an authority to serve and build up.

4. He is able to deal with the diverse unique situations in the various leadership situations in such a way as to demonstrate the presence and power of the Lord.

5. He is able to utilize his experience based ministry philosophy to turn each of the leadership situations into potential avenues for growth, for both himself and the people in the situations.

Doohan points out strengths and weaknesses of Pauline leadership.

MAJOR IMPLICATIONS OF DOOHAN INCLUDE:

1. An analysis of Pauline leadership points out what modern leadership theorists are now finding, that there is no best leadership style and no best strategy for change. Leaders must adapt to the dynamics of the leadership basal elements of leader, followers, situation, and other dynamic elements that we assert in our complex contingency model of leadership at the School of World Mission.

2. Paul's leadership response highlights the fact that crisis can lead to growth for all concerned. Theological input must govern the facilitation of the appropriate responses of followers.

3. Atmosphere between leaders and followers is crucial in terms of what can be done in a leadership situation. Doohan notes that Paul could do certain things in situations where the leader-follower relationships were better and where he could not. She challenges modern day leaders to create the types of atmospheres seen in those positive leadership situations of Paul.

4. Every leader will be unique with varying dominant characteristics. Paul certainly was.

CONCLUDING REMARKS

It is impossible to summarize very well Doohan's conclusions. She writes so eloquently with terseness and implications that call for deep reflection. This browsing effort showed the necessity of going back and getting the in-depth analysis of each of the chapters. Yes, this browsing showed that the book is definitely worthy of further serious study.

2. Decision For Further Reading

    a. The book should be read for thematic intent at the following evaluation read level:

        ___ (1) pre-read level

        _x_ (2) in-depth read level

        _x_ (3) study level

    b. No further reading needed

This book should be read at least at in-depth read level and maybe at study level. It is an outstanding book reflecting scholarship and Christian values.

OUTLINE SHEET FOR BROWSE READING

Name of Person Doing Browse Reading:

Name of Book:

Unit Being Browsed:

____ 1. paragraphs: identify larger unit

____ 2. chapter sections (a consecutive group of paragraphs relating to a major idea of a chapter): identify extent of chapter section.

____ 3. whole chapters: identify which ones:

____ 4. parts of a section of a book (several chapters developing some single aspect of a major idea of a section of a book): Identify extent of the parts of the section:

____ 5. sections of a book (entire groups of chapters developing a major idea of the thesis of the book). Identify extent of the section:

____ 6. the whole book.

Time Involved:

1. Note any observations of ideas, relevant insights, illustrations, biblical exegesis, quotes or other information useful to you. Where important, you may wish to identify the unit being browsed along with the relevant information.

2. Decision For Further Reading: A. The book should be read for thematic intent at the following evaluation read level:

____ (1) pre-read level

____ (2) in-depth read level

____ (3) study level b.

____ No further reading needed

FEEDBACK ON BROWSE READING

1. What is the essential difference between browsing and ransacking?

___ a. ransacking is a comparative methodology while browsing is a speed reading technique

___ b. ransacking is a speed reading technique while browsing is a comparative methodology

___ c. ransacking is a contextual methodology while browsing is a comparative methodology

___ d. ransacking is a comparative methodology while browsing is a contextual methodology.

2. Read again the three major results of browsing reading.

THREE RESULTS

When you have browsed through a book you will be able to :

___ (1) Answer evaluation type questions on the limited portion of the book which you read such as:

- what did the author say?

- how well did he/she say it?

- what did he/she leave unsaid?

- how does this book compare with something else?

- how useful is it?

___ (2) Place the limited portion being browsed in the total context of the book so as not to misperceive the author's intent.

___ (3) Decide whether or not your interpretation of the limited portion will require you to pre-read or in-depth read the book for thematic content or structural intent.

Which of these three results do you think will be the most difficult to arrive at? Check the one that is most difficult for you.

ANSWERS ——1. x d.

2. Your choice. For me x (2) is the most difficult since I am reading in-depth a portion of the whole. x (3) is a close second. When reading only a selective portion, it is easy to read out of context out of the book as a whole and thus misperceive the author's intent.

Pre-Reading

Introduction

Pre-reading a book is a sign of serious intent to understand an entire book. When you pre-read a book, you are seeking to find out the overall thematic content of the book and to see how the author is structuring his/her material to develop the thematic intent. You pre-read a book when in your scanning, ransacking, or browsing you determine that the book is well written and has developed an important topic in an organized manner. In pre-reading a book, you will be doing your best to identify a single statement of what the author is saying without reading the entire book. It is a special kind of survey which takes careful thinking and extrapolation based on limited amount of information. The skills to do this are developed only with practice. After you have pre-read several books and then have followed with reading and discovered how well your pre-reading agrees or disagrees with your reading, you will develop skill and confidence in your ability to pre-read.

Definition

Pre-reading a book is a special kind of survey of a book which involves drawing implications from various portions of the book as to the thematic and structural intent of the book.

Comment

Thematic intent refers to a single statement that weaves together the main subject of the book and each major idea developed about the book.

Comment

Structural intent refers to a recognition of how the author uses each portion of the book to contribute to the subject or major ideas of the book.

Four Results

When you have pre-read a book you will have tentative statements describing:

1. The kind of book being pre-read,
2. The author's intent and methodology,
3. The author's thesis which involves the major subject and supporting major ideas,
4. The intent of each major section (or minor where necessary) and how they contribute to the thesis statement.

Example

See following page for an example of pre-reading using C. Peter Wagner's, **Church Growth and the Whole Gospel.**

Example of Pre-Reading a Book

Book: Church Growth and the Whole Gospel, by C. Peter Wagner

Descriptive Statement

CG &TWG is an "extended position paper" describing how the Church Growth Movement now relates to a number of criticisms and/or issues which it did not adequately treat in the past. It is written in an open, personal, warm, popular style which seeks to bridge opponents rather than to cut them off.

Author's Intent

For a tentative statement of author's intent and methodology, see **The Church Growth Bulletin** (March-April 1982) where the author discusses this point. The author also gives his intent in his introduction to the book.

Tentative Thesis Statement

Subject:
Church Growth Theory Supports a Holistic Gospel

Major Ideas

- by stressing a double mandate (cultural and evangelistic) which includes conversion in the social context and cultural context,
- though it prioritizes the evangelistic mandate and individual conversion over change of social structures and context;
- which recognizes the contextually of ethics and barriers to conversion
- suggest that unique structures can symbiotically best fulfill both mandates.

STRUCTURAL INTENT

It appears that the author uses his structure as follows:

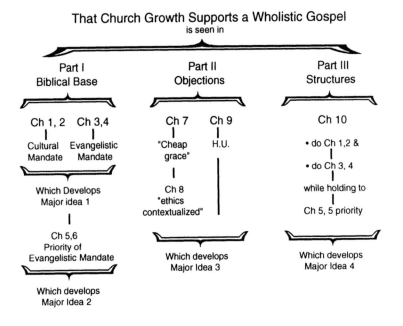

That Church Growth Supports a Wholistic Gospel
is seen in

Part I Biblical Base	Part II Objections	Part III Structures

Ch 1, 2   Ch 3,4

Cultural   Evangelistic
Mandate   Mandate

Which Develops
Major idea 1

Ch 5,6
Priority of
Evangelistic Mandate

Which develops
Major Idea 2

Ch 7   Ch 9

"Cheap   H.U.
grace"

Ch 8
"ethics
contextualized"

Which develops
Major Idea 3

Ch 10

• do Ch 1,2 &

• do Ch 3, 4

while holding to

Ch 5, 5 priority

Which develops
Major Idea 4

How to Pre-Read a Book

Introduction

Pre-reading a book is a sign of serious intent to understand an entire book. When you pre-read a book you are seeking to find out the overall thematic content of the book and to see how the author is structuring his/her material to develop the thematic intent. You pre-read a book when in your scanning, ransacking or browsing you determine that the book is well written and has developed an important topic in an organized manner. In pre-reading a book, you will be doing your best to identify a single statement of what the author is saying without reading the entire book. It is a special kind of survey which takes careful thinking and extrapolation based on limited amount of information. The following steps will help you in your efforts to pre-read a book.

Major Task

Glean from the introductory material and summary-like information enough knowledge about the book to be able to formulate five statements about the book before you actually read it.

Five statements

The end result of your pre-reading will be:

1. A statement describing the kind of book being pre-read.

2. A statement giving the author's intent and methodology.

3. A single statement which identifies the major subject and weaves it together with the major ideas developed about the subject in the book.

4. A series of statements indicating the intent of each major section (or minor where necessary) and its contribution to either the major subject of the book or major ideas about the book.

5. An evaluation of miscellaneous helps available.

How To Pre-Read A Book

Step	Procedure
1	Examine The Title and Subtitle (if given) and Suggest What They Indicate About the Book Itself – such as: • kind of material • kind of book • methodology used • intent of book • main subject of the book • thematic intent of the book
2	Examine the Forward (if given) and observe what is said about the book by someone else. A careful examination will often reveal: • statement of purpose • statement of theme • evaluation of how well the author carried out his/her intent • identification of the main subject of the book • significant contributions of the book • summary-like descriptions of the book
3	Examine the preface or introduction (if given) for the author's own statement of: • intent • main subject and major ideas • methodology for accomplishing his/her purposes • presuppostions • structuring of the book
4	Examine the table of contents: a. If the author divides the book into large sections, complete the following sentence for each section: "It looks as though the author is going to ... in this section." Comment: In a well organized book, a major section will develop a main idea about the subject of the book b. Repeat the same procedure for each chapter in the book, ie. answer the following question: "It looks as though the author is going to... in the chapter." Comment: If the author does not organize chapters into sections, you will have to identify the major ideas yourself by grouping chapters from your statements of intent of each chapter. Usually several chapters go together to deal with a major idea. If the table of contents is not well organized, you should dip into the chapters hurriedly to obtain these statements. You can do this by looking at "cue headings" summaries and chapter questions, etc.
5	If the book has a dust cover, write down any information given there that you have not previously learned. Comment: "dust cover" refers to the publicity jacket that libraries usually leave on books. This jacket often has information on the front or back flaps describing briefly what the book is about, and a short description of the author and the perspective from which he/she is approaching his/her subject. While usually of a superficial nature can often be helpful in "guessing" the author's major subject. If you are reading a thesis be sure and read the "vita" as this will always give helpful information concerning the author.
6	Examine the various reference helps including indicies, bibliography, footnotes, glossary, etc. and familiarize yourself with these helps before you actually get into the text. Comment: The reference helps will often give very helpful information concerning major subject and major ideas. Appendices often deal with various sub-ideas involved in major ideas.

OUTLINE SHEET FOR PRE-READING A BOOK

Person Doing Pre-Read: **Date:**

Author:

Title of Book:

1. Give here your statement describing the kind of book you pre-read. (See Step 1, page 38 for details of how to do this.)

2. Give here a statement describing the author's intent and methodology for carrying out that intent. (See Step 3, page 38 which is the primary help, and Steps 2 and 5 which sometimes help, page 38.)

3. Give here a single statement which clearly identifies the main subject of the book and weaves that subject to the major ideas developed about the subject. (Steps 1-5 all help do this.) Be sure that your major subject is clearly identified and that each major idea is clearly seen in its relationship to the major subject.

4. Give here your series of statements indicating how the author uses the structure of the book to develop his/her thesis statement identified in Step 3 above. (Step 4 helps on this, page 38.) Use the back of the sheet if more room is necessary.

5. Evaluate the miscellaneous helps in the book (i.e. various reference helps, such as indices, bibliography, footnotes, glossary, appendices, etc.).

Feedback on Pre-Reading a Book

1. Which of the following are characteristic of a pre-read? (Check any that apply)

_____ a. A serious committal to the evaluation side of the reading continuum.

_____ b. It presupposes a scan, ransack and thorough enough browse to do reflective thinking concerning the integration of the book.

_____ c. It assumes an integrated coherent well written book.

_____ d. It is a special kind of survey which requires careful thinking and extrapolation based on limited amount of information.

_____ e. Is a skill which develops with experience.

2. Glance again at the major task of a pre-read. *Glean from the introductory material and summary-like information enough knowledge about the book to be able to formulate five statements about the book before you actually read it.* (You may want to go back and re-read the five statements you have to formulate.)

What is meant by "introductory material and summary-like information?" Check any of the below items which fit these descriptions.

_____ a. Appendices

_____ b. Indices

_____ c. Title and Sub-Title

_____ d. Foreword

_____ e. Preface

_____ f. Introduction

_____ g. Table of Contents

_____ h. Dust Cover

_____ i. Chapter Summaries

_____ j. Conclusion Section to Book

3. Check below which of the four items you think will be most difficult for you. What do you think will be the major hindrances to your arriving at each of the four statements required by a pre-read?

_____ (1) A statement describing the kind of book being pre-read.

_____ (2) A statement giving the author's intent and methodology.

_____ (3) A single statement which identifies the major subject and weaves it together with the major ideas developed about the subject in the book.

_____ (4) A series of statements indicating the intent of each major section (or minor where necessary) and its contribution to either the major subject of the book or major ideas about the book.

ANSWERS

1. x a, x b, x c, x d, x e; (I certainly hope this last one is true.)

2. x c, x d, x e, x f, x g, x h, x i, x j;

3. Usually for most students, item 3, a single concise integrating statement of the author's theme interwoven with his/her major ideas, is the most difficult. One, they have never been taught to see a book as a whole and to see its structure as accomplishing an overall thematic intent. Two, many books are not organized coherently nor written to integrate some major thematic idea. For (1) students are not used to seeing books as different kinds of books (how to, motivational, scholarly, market oriented, collection of isolated issues, etc.) For (2) if no preface or introduction is given then intent must be dug out of the book itself. It is usually buried in aside comments or footnotes. For (3) it is hard work weaving complex ideas into a single encompassing statement. Students would rather write a longer descriptive paragraph. For (4) it is the actual identification of the Parts (and Sections) which is difficult along with ability to concisely summarize.

An in-depth Reading of a Book

syn: detailed reading, hard read

Introduction

You do an in-depth read of a book when you have determined from scanning, ransacking, and browsing that it is worth pre-reading and reading. Reading a book is a serious detailed approach to the understanding of what the author is saying. It is an approach which says that the book deserves to be read in a detailed enough way so you are able to give evaluation statements about the book as a whole. When you have read a book you have an overall grasp of the book and can discuss it motivationally with a potential reader. You will be able to discuss six kinds of evaluation statements which are described below.

Definition

An *in-depth reading* of a book is a detailed approach to the evaluation of a book which involves pre-reading followed by detailed reading of all parts of the text in order to affirm, deny or modify the pre-reading analysis and to produce six evaluation statements.

A Major Result

When you have read a book you will have determined the validity of your pre-reading and will have modified it if necessary to fit the facts of your detailed reading. This means you will have firm statements describing: A. the kind of book it is; B. the author's intent and methodology; C. the author's thesis which involves a single unifying statement connecting the main subject of the book with its supporting major ideas; D. the way the book structurally develops its thesis.

Six Evaluation Statements

When you've done a detailed read of a book, you will be able to identify the following kinds of evaluation statements. You will have, if appropriate,

1. Shown where the author is uninformed in his/her writing, (i.e. examples from the book where the author draws conclusions without considering all the facts).

2. Shown where the author is misinformed in his/her writing, (i.e. instances/examples from the book in which the author draws conclusions based on false information).

3. Shown where the author is illogical in his/her writing, (i.e. examples from the book in which the author uses faulty reasoning in arriving at conclusions) .

4. Shown where the author's analysis or account is incomplete in terms of his/her statement of purpose in writing the book, (i.e. an evaluation of the author's accomplishment of purpose in writing the book).

5. Shown the author's strengths in his/her writing, (i.e. reference to useful quotations, point out any strong arguments or explanations, point out concepts which can be transferred to your own experience).

6. Shown the relevance of the book to today's needs, (i.e. applications to various life-situations to which the book can be applied. You can point out the kind of reader who will profit the most by the book).

HOW TO DO AN IN-DEPTH READ OF A BOOK

INTRODUCTION

The kind of reading described under "detailed reading" applies to reading in which the intent is that of learning. It is serious reading for scholarly purposes. You will discover that most books you read can be done by scanning, ransacking, browsing and pre-reading. Few books require using the read or study styles of reading.

HOW TO DO AN IN-DEPTH READ OF A BOOK

Step	Procedure	Details
1	Pre-read the book.	1. Use the Pre-reading Procedures (Page 38) to get the five pre-reading analysis statements.
2	Determine the author's purpose in writing the book.	1. Summarize into a concise statement what you found in your pre-reading concerning the book. 2. As you read through the text, look for any restatements, clarifications, or enlargements of the author's purpose. 3. If the author's purpose is not stated in the book, then compose your own idea of it.
3	Determine the author's overall thought in the book (i.e. the *thesis statement* for the book).	1. As you complete the reading of each chapter, summarize the main thought of the chapter in a single sentence. 2. As you complete the reading of each section, summarize the main thought of the section in a single sentence. 3. When you complete the whole book, summarize the main subject of the book into a single, comprehensive statement to which each of the individual parts can be related. This may involve synthesizing a major subject of the book and relating it to each of the major ideas developed in each section.
4	Evaluate the book.	1. Read through the text in detail in order to formulate the evaluation statements described in the "How To Evaluate A Book Table" on page 46. 2. Not all evaluations may apply to a given book. At your present level of understanding, you may not be able to do evaluations, but where evaluations can be done, be sure you make them concise.
5	Write up what you have discovered in your detailed reading of the book.	1. You have done a good piece of work when you have completed a "detailed reading." You should profit rom your reading by writing a review which others will find profitable. 2. Use the "How To Write A Review" procedure on page 55, 56.

FEEDBACK ON HOW TO DO AN IN-DEPTH READING OF A BOOK

1. What is the essential difference between a pre-read and an in-depth read?

   ____ a. The pre-read simply summarizes the results of the scan, browse, and ransack reading while the in-depth reading evaluates the author's accomplishment in terms of purpose, theme, analysis, and relevance.

   ____ b. The pre-read is a preliminary attempt to identify the author's thematic attempt and structural means for accomplishing that intent. The in-depth read is a full blown evaluation of the results of the pre-read thematic identification, plus evaluation of how well the author actually did accomplish his/her purposes.

   ____ c. There is no essential difference in the two.

   ____ d. None of the above.

2. Note again evaluation statements 1 and 2. What might be a major hindrance to carrying out the analysis required by them? (hint: What common item is implied in both of them?)

   (1) Show where the author is uninformed in his/her writing, (i.e. examples from the book where the author draws conclusions without considering all the facts).

   (2) Show where the author is misinformed in his/her writing, (i.e. instances/examples from the book in which the author draws conclusions based on false information).

3. Which of the remaining evaluation statements will, generally speaking, be the most difficult for you personally? Check and explain.

   ____ (3) Show where the author is illogical in his/her writing (i.e. examples from the book in which the author uses faulty reasoning in arriving at conclusions).

   ____ (4) Show where the author's analysis or account is incomplete in terms of his/her statement of purpose in writing the book, (i.e. an evaluation of the author's accomplishment of purpose in writing the book).

___ (5) Show the author's strengths in his/her writing
(i.e. reference to useful quotations, point out any strong
arguments or explanations, point out concepts which can
be transferred to your own experience).

___ (6) Show the relevance of the book to today's needs, (i.e.
applications to various life-situations to which the book
can be applied. You can point out the kind of reader who
will profit the most by the book).

ANSWERS

1. x b; 2. The reader must have some outside knowledge of the
subject involved in order to know if the author is misinformed or uninformed. On a subject in which a reader has little knowledge, these two
evaluations will be difficult if not impossible; 3. Here is my general
opinion based on what students have done in the past: (5) is relatively
easy for most, (3) is most difficult, (4) is usually not done very well, and
(6) is more difficult than it sounds since books of in-depth read are
usually more toward the abstract than practical side, hence more readers have more difficulty in transferring ideas to real life situations.

DETAILED READING - HOW TO EVALUATE A BOOK

INTRODUCTION

When you have read a book, you should have an overall grasp of it
and be able to discuss it motivationally with a potential reader. That is,
you should be able to persuade a potential reader as to the value (or lack
of value) in reading it. The six evaluation statements below provide a
basis for you to talk intelligently to potential readers about the book.

HOW TO EVALUATE A BOOK

Step	Procedure
1	Examine The Title and Subtitle (if given) and Suggest What They Indicate About the Book Itself – such as: • kind of material • kind of book • methodology used • intent of book • main subject of the book • thematic intent of the book

How To Evaluate A Book Cont.

Step	Procedure
2	Examine the Forward (if given) and observe what is said about the book by someone else. A careful examination will often reveal: • statement of purpose • statement of theme • evaluation of how well the author carried out his/her intent • identification of the main subject of the book • significant contributions of the book • summary-like descriptions of the book
3	Examine the preface or introduction (if given) for the author's own statement of: • intent • main subject and major ideas • methodology for accomplishing his/her purposes • presuppostions • structuring of the book
4	**Examine the table of contents:** a. If the author divides the book into large sections, complete the following sentence for each section: "It looks as though the author is going to ... in this section." **Comment:** In a well organized book, a major section will develop a main idea about the subject of the book b. Repeat the same procedure for each chapter in the book, ie. answer the following question: "It looks as though the author is going to... in the chapter." **Comment:** If the author does not organize chapters into sections, you will have to identify the major ideas yourself by grouping chapters from your statements of intent of each chapter. Usually several chapters go together to deal with a major idea. If the table of contents is not well organized, you should dip into the chapters hurriedly to obtain these statements. You can do this by looking at "cue headings" summaries and chapter questions, etc.
5	If the book has a dust cover, write down any information given there that you have not previously learned. **Comment:** "dust cover" refers to the publicity jacket that libraries usually leave on books. This jacket often has information on the front or back flaps describing briefly what the book is about, and a short description of the author and the perspective from which he/she is approaching his/her subject. While usually of a superficial nature can often be helpful in "guessing" the author's major subject. If you are reading a thesis be sure and read the "vita" as this will always give helpful information concerning the author.
6	Examine the various reference helps including indicies, bibliography, footnotes, glossary, etc. and familiarize yourself with these helps before you actually get into the text. **Comment:** The reference helps will often give very helpful information concerning major subject and major ideas. Appendices often deal with various sub-ideas involved in major ideas.

OUTLINE SHEET FOR AN IN-DEPTH READING OF A BOOK

Person Doing In-Depth Read: Date:

Author:

Title of Book:

1. Give the results of your pre-reading the above book for your statement of the author's thesis (a single statement which clearly identifies the main subject of the book and weaves that subject to the major idea developed about the subject. Be sure that your major subject is clearly identified and that each major idea is clearly seen in its relationship to the major subject. Use back of sheet if more room is needed for answer).

2. Give your evaluation statements concerning the following items. (If an evaluation statement does not apply - say so.) (Use the back of this sheet to continue your answers to the following questions when necessary.)

a. Examples where the author is uninformed: (See Step 1, page 46)

b. Examples where the author is misinformed: (See Step 2, page 47)

c. Examples where the author is illogical: (See Step 3, page 47)

d. Examples where the author is incomplete in terms of purpose: (See Step 4, page 47)

e. Strengths in the book: (See Step 5, page 47)

f. Relevance of the book: (See Step 6, page 47)

Feedback on Evaluating a Book

1. Read again the 6 steps in doing detailed reading. How many of the steps are essentially negative in orientation? How many positive?

2. Why are the negative steps important?

3. What is the essential importance of the positive steps?

4. Which of the 6 are most in harmony with the intent underlying the sub-title of this booklet?

Answers

1. Steps 1 through 4 are essentially negative in intent (Uniformed, Misinformed, Illogical, Purpose). They are to analyze critically whether the author has not done what he/she intended. Steps 5 and 6 are positive. They seek to get out of the book that which can be useful.

2. The negative steps are important for corrective reasons. We should not recommend for use principles, applications, models, etc. which do not hold under close scrutiny.

3. They highlight getting the usefulness out of a book.

4. The sub-title indicates that the major purpose of reading (at least in terms of the purposes underlying this booklet) is to read selectively in order to acquire information for use. Steps 4 and 5 are focused on that very purpose.

STUDYING A BOOK

INTRODUCTION

Studying a book requires the most detailed kind of reading. It involves first pre-reading and reading the book. But it also involves the ability to do comparative evaluations and original research on materials and ideas used in the book.

DEFINITION

Studying a book is a special in-depth approach to the reading of a book which involves pre-reading, reading, and background research on materials and ideas used in the book.

SIX RESULTS

When you have studied a book you will:

1. Have done the four pre-reading statements,

2. Have arrived at appropriate evaluation statements from the six evaluation statements normally considered in detailed reading,

3. Be able to discuss the book analytically with another reader,

4. Be able to evaluate the other reader's analysis for clarification, modification, etc.,

5. Have researched original materials quoted in the book for evaluating accuracy,

6. Be able to compare the book with other books dealing with the same major subject so as to show similarities, differences, unique contributions, etc.

COMMENT

Due to the nature of the in-depth work involved in "study reading" you will usually limit this kind of reading to:

- Essential works which will significantly effect your ministry (basal books in your field).

- Works which are complex in concepts and/or structure and which usually require more than several read-throughs.

COMMENT

Not all leaders are capable of this kind of in-depth approach to reading nor do they have available time to do this kind of study. People in this situation should identify resource centers and/or people who do this kind of reading and can be trusted to give reliable reports. Organizations should seek to create their own research centers where this kind of necessary study can be done on behalf of the organization.

EXAMPLES

Books such as the following are probably worthy of the "study approach" to reading if you are at the SWM studying missiology:

- The 1981 revised edition of McGavran's **Understanding Church Growth,**
- Kraft's **Christianity in Culture.**

COMMENT

This booklet does not treat the study aspect of the continuum in an in-depth fashion. Most books read by busy leaders will be at lesser levels. For further help on in-depth study reading see Mortimer J. Adler's latest edition of **How To Read A Book.**

Basal Books

Introduction

I have found it helpful when reading items in a given category to first identify a *basal* (basic, foundational, seminal) *book* for the category. A basal book treats the category thoroughly from a theoretical perspective. Such a book can be used as a standard when reading other material in the category. I read the basal book somewhat carefully in order to get one theoretical framework. I can then afford to scan, browse, or ransack other entries in the category by way of comparing, contrasting, noting significant differences or modifications.

Description

A *basal book* is a book which covers a given category of interest in such a way as to provide a standard for comparing, contrasting, and generally understanding other books covering aspects of that same category.

Comment

One way to identify a basal book is to note how frequently author's refer to it or quote from it or use major definitions and categorizations derived from it.

Comment

Frequently others will suggest or recommend a book as being an important book. These should be thought of as potential basal books. Words like essential, seminal in the field are cues.

Examples

In the leadership field, I have found it helpful to utilize the following leadership categories of interest to me. Table 1 lists some of the basal materials I have identified thus far:

TABLE 1. BASAL BOOKS IN LEADERSHIP FIELD[1]

CATEGORY	BASAL BOOK OR ARTICLE
1. Theory	Yukl (1981)
2. History	Clinton (1986a)
3. Philosophy	Greenleaf (1977), Hodgkinson (1983)
4. Transformational	Life-History, Clinton (1989)
5. Trait Theory	Stogdill (1948)
6. Contingency Models	Hershey and Blanchard (1977)
7. Follower Element	Hollander (1978)
8. Christian Perspectives	Doohan (1984)
9. Power and Authority	Wrong (1980)
10. Organizational Dynamics	Mintzberg (1976)
11. Change Dynamics	Havelock (1973)
12. Leadership Styles	Clinton (1986b)
13. Leadership Research	Hunt and Larson (1977)

COMMENT

I am suggesting, in introducing to you the concept of basal book, that you should:

1.   Identify major categories of interest to you in your ministry.

2.   Be constantly on the lookout for basal books.

3.   Ask other leaders to identify for you their basal books.

FEEDBACK ON STUDYING AND BASAL BOOKS

1.   What is the essential difference between an in-depth reading of a book and studying a book?

_____ a.   An in-depth read primarily focuses on the book itself in terms of its evaluation, while a study approach goes beyond the book itself to its basic sources and other comparative experts in the field.

---

[1] See the bibliography section for an annotated listing of the basal materials shown in Table 1.

___ b. An in-depth read is evaluatory in nature while a study approach is more surface in its analysis.

___ c. There is no essential difference

___ d. None of the above - you describe.

2. What kind of books should be books chosen for study purposes?

3. List some categories of interest to you for which you would like to identify basal books.

4. Name some basal books you have already identified.[2]

ANSWERS

1. x a.
2. Books which are well organized and develop an important theme or are important to your field. These basal books should deal with fundamental issues and various aspects of your ministry.
3. I am interested in identifying basal books for the following categories: theological treatment of influence, power, and authority; biographical writing theory; leadership accountability.
4. Besides the leadership fields I have previously listed, I'm interested in and have identified basal books in hermeneutics, prayer, spiritual gifts, spiritual authority, personal development, grounded theory research.

---

[2] You should recognize that you will identify a basal book which gets you started in a given field. Later you may find a more adequate basal book. The essential idea of a basal book is "root information" that you can use for comparison purposes when reading in a given aspect of a field. A person reads with much more efficiency when reading with some knowledge of a subject and reading to confirm, modify, or alter what is already known about a subject.

How To Write A Review
From A Detailed Reading

Introduction

When you have taken the time to pre-read and read a book, you have invested several hours. One way to recoup your investment of time is to write a review whereby others may learn from your experience. The following suggestions assume that you have pre-read and read a book using the basic procedures described previously.

How To Write A Review

Task	Description
1	*Write an opening paragraph which includes the kind of book it is, the author's purpose, thesis, and style.* Detailed procedures: 1. Examine your analysis of the book and isolate the facts you need for this paragraph. 2. Include in this paragraph items from the book which demonstrate these facts. (This is optinal - depending on the length you want in the opening paragraph and whether or not the ook lends itself well to this). 3. Arrange this material into a short paragraph. 4. Close the paragraph with a transitional sentence leading into paragraph two.
2	*Write a paragraph which describes the basic contents of the book.* Detailed procedures: 1. If the author uses sections or chapters use your section and chapter descriptions to show the basic content of the book. 2. Mention any significant portions of the book which form a valuable sub-topic in the book.
3	*Write a paragraph which gives your critical view of the author's success in accomplishing his/her purpose.* Detailed procedures: 1. State your conclusion as to the unity of the book and the relevance of each section to the author's purpose. 2. Point out particular weaknesses and strengths in the author's thought process. 3. State your opinion as to whether or not the author accomplished his/her purpose. Include the reasons for your judgement, when applicable.

How To Write A Review cont.

Task	Description
4	**Write a paragraph which describes the mechanics of the layout of the book.** Detailed procedures: 1. Examine the various reference helps including indices, table of contents, bibliography, footnotes, glossary, etc. Make a statement as to their usefulness or their deficiencies. Point out what other reference aids were not available, but would have enhanced the usefulness of the book. 2. Examine the preface, intorduction, or forward to determine if any outstanding help from them should be mentioned. 3. Evaluate the readability of the book in terms of its printing, layout, use of illustrations, charts, maps, etc.
5	**Write a concluding paragraph which describes the relevance of the book and your personal recommendations as to how the book should be used.** Detailed procedures: 1. Examine your evaluation of the book and isolate the needed facts. 2. Summarize your findings in such a way that your recommendation regarding the book will be clear.

CONCLUSION - SOME FOLLOW-UP SUGGESTIONS

There are different purposes in reading books. One can read for pleasure. Pleasure reading requires word by word reading, even reflection on: choice of words, descriptive phrases, sentences and paragraph construction. It is a meditative reflective process in which one gets engrossed in the author's presentation. Or one can read in order to take a test in the material of a book. For such detailed reading it is important to analyze, note significant factual intent, look at implications of cue headings, etc.[3] For one must be able to recall and interact with most of the content. Or one can read to obtain useful information. To obtain useful information does not require that one get lost in word-by-word reading or constructing lists of information to be repeated. Instead, reading for information requires the ability to overview, extrapolate, draw implications, move rapidly through material looking for selected ideas, etc. In short, the purpose of reading should control the reading methodology.

The thrust of this booklet suggests that books being read for information should be approached differently. Some books should be

---

[3] A book like QUEST gives an adequate approach for "test reading." See bibliography.

overviewed in a cursory fashion; others must be given in-depth treatment. The nature of the book being read and the purpose for reading it
will determine the level in the reading continuum that should apply.
The end result of reading, using continuum reading concepts, is acquisition of useful information.   You have read an entertainment book
when you finish it. You have read a book on which you are tested when
you are prepared for the test. Both of those types of approaches usually
require reading all the words, and all the pages, and all the chapters in
the book. Not so with continuum reading. You have read a book using
continuum reading concepts when you have assessed the level it should
be read at and you read only as much as necessary at that level to obtain
useful information from the book.

The implications of this approach are several. You should recognize that you will read many books at assessment levels (scan, ransack,
and browse) and fewer at evaluation levels (pre-read, read, study). This
means you need to become very proficient in skills associated with assessment levels of reading. It means, too, that you must learn to become highly selective in books to be read at evaluation levels. That
further implies that you should formulate categories of interest and identify crucial books (basal books) for these categories.

In doing comparative studies in leaders' lives, I have been able to
generalize some important leadership lessons. Here is one which the
concepts and skills in this book support.

Effective Leaders Maintain A Learning Posture Throughout Their Lives.

One major way effective leaders (in societies where literacy is important) manifest this learning posture is through reading. Frequently,
God significantly affects a leader through some interaction with written ideas. This is such a common happening that the process has been
given a name and described in detail (Clinton 1987: 180, 181). In
leadership development theory, this is called a literary process item.
Now, leaders should recognize this important means of God's development in their lives and deliberately use it. A closing suggestion involves
use of an accountability model, the *Buddy-Reading Model,* to help you
do just this.

Buddy Reading Model

Introduction

In the book by Hendricks which I used as an example for closed ransacking, Teaching To Change Lives, I was struck by one of Hendricks' observations. He pointed out that many people are reading a lot but not seeing much effect from it (1987: 25). He suggests that they read but do not reflect on it. The various suggestions for the levels of reading are designed to make you do just that, to reflect on what you are reading. The idea of selective reading forces reflection and hence, increases the potential use of ideas which will indeed bring about changes in your life and ministry. A second item which can insure learning is to have some accountability for what you are reading. The essence of the model is commitment to reading with a friend or colleague in such a way that you are accountable to that friend for reading and learning. The model was suggested to me by Mike Jaffarian on one of my trips to Singapore. He has been using the model for years. I call it the buddy reading model. I have now applied the model and actually have several reading buddies.

Description

The *buddy reading* model is a high commitment, high accountability model for continued learning through reading in which two people:

- alternately select a book to read (that is, one person selects a book for both to read; once that book has been read, the other person selects the next book that both will read),

- meet on a regular basis to discuss the results of the reading assignments,

- agree on assignments for each book,

- hold each other accountable for doing the assignments, learning from them, applying what has been learned.

ADVANTAGES

Three advantages of this model are readily suggested:

- accountability—you will continue to read and have outside help on evaluating your learning,

- diversity - the alternate choice of books insures that you will be forced to tackle new subject areas that you would not normally approach,

- exposure to other ideas—even though you are reading the same book you will not see the same things; hence, you will expose your buddy to ideas you saw and your buddy will do the same for you.

REGULARITY

The model allows for meeting on any kind of regular basis. Some people meet once a week. Some meet once a month. Some once every two months.

ASSIGNMENTS

Usually, the person who chooses the book for the current time suggests what assignment should be done. Or, you can use a common assignment which you apply to all the books you use. I will suggest an outline that can be used in that way.

OUTLINE FORM FOR BUDDY READING MODEL

INTRODUCTION

The following common assignment is used for any book chosen. Note that it uses continuum reading concepts discussed in this booklet. My reading buddy, Denny Repko, and I are interested in using what we learn with others. Thus, the heavy emphasis on mentoring (see Item 5).[4]

OUTLINE SHEET FOR BUDDY READING MODEL

1. Results of Continuum Overview - At what level should a book be read? (Attach Scan, Browse, Ransack results if applicable - otherwise note how book should be read)

2. Note items from the book which should be permanently filed for future use like quotes, illustrations, major ideas, diagrams, models, scripture exegesis or insights, etc., where filed, how filed.
   Marked in book ___ yes ___ no

3. Evaluation insights of book: (limitations, weaknesses, strengths). See also DETAILED READING - HOW TO EVALUATE A BOOK (uninformed, misinformed, illogical, purpose, strengths, relevance)

4. Determine Subject Classification (what about, what type of book)

5. Mentoring Assessment. Determine mentoring follow-up:
   a. recommend for (what, who in general):
   b. write to:
   c. use with:

6. Immediate Personal Follow-up:

7. General Long Term Follow-up:

8. Miscellaneous (anything else not already covered):

---

[4] See **Connecting** by Stanley and Clinton, 1992, and **The Mentor Handbook** by Clinton and Clinton, 1991, for further information on mentoring. Both of these entries are annotated in the bibliography.

BIBLIOGRAPHY FOR READING ON THE RUN

Adler, Mortimer J.

    1967   HOW TO READ A BOOK - THE ART OF GETTING A LIBERAL EDUCATION. New York: Simon and Schuster.

Comments: This was the edition I studied years ago. There is a later revised edition.

Bass, Bernard M.

    1981   STOGDILL'S HANDBOOK OF LEADERSHIP; A Survey of Theory and Research. New York: The Free Press.

Comments: Era—Written during the latter stages of the Contingency Era. Why Significant—This is the most comprehensive text out on leadership theory. It surveys leadership from its earliest beginnings and displays findings as well as gives interpretive comments about the findings. It has a bibliographic section with over 5000 entries in it.

Bogardus, Emory S.

    1934   LEADERS AND LEADERSHIP. New York: Appleton-Century-Crofts Inc.

Comments: Used as scan example and open ransack example.

Clinton, J. R.

    1986a   A SHORT HISTORY OF LEADERSHIP THEORY—A PARADIGMATIC OVERVIEW OF THE FIELD OF LEADERSHIP FROM 1841 TO 1986. Altadena: Barnabas Publishers.

Comments: This surveys the leadership field from the mid1800s to the present. It identifies the major boundaries between paradigms, identifies dominant models for each phase, prominent works for each phase, and prominent influentials as well as defines 11 important models or theories during this historical period.

Clinton, J. R.
    1986b   LEADERSHIP STYLES. Altadena: Barnabas Publishers.
Comments: This booklet views leadership style as an individual expression a leader utilizes to influence in a variety of leadership acts such as handling crises, problem solving, decision making, forming and maintaining interpersonal relationships, and using shades of persuasion techniques. 10 biblical styles on a continuum from highly directive to highly non-directive are examined. The thrust of this article is toward recognition of the need for multi-styled leadership.

Clinton, J. R.
    1987   LEADERSHIP EMERGENCE THEORY. Altadena: Barnabas
             Publishers. (latest version out is 1989).
Comments: A leader's life is analyzed in terms of major development phases, boundary processing, and process items God uses to develop that leader in character and ministry and in terms of sphere of influence for which God holds that leader accountable.

Clinton, J. R. and Clinton, R.W.
    1991   THE MENTOR HANDBOOK. Altadena: Barnabas Pub-
             lishers.
Comments: This is a detailed manual for use by mentors to sharpen the focus of their mentoring. This has all you want to know about mentoring and more.

Cohen, Ruth; King, Wayne; Knudsvig, Glenn; Markel, Geralding Ponte; Patten, David; Shtogren, John; Wilhelm, Rowena May
    1973   QUEST: ACADEMIC SKILLS PROGRAM. New York:
             Harcourt Brace Jovanovich.

Comments: This book teaches students how to read and mark books for taking tests. It also exposes all kinds of skills for test taking.

Doohan, Helen
1984   LEADERSHIP IN PAUL. Wilmington, Delaware: Michael
          Glazier, Inc.
Comments: A person well-read in leadership theory in general who is
able to apply those perspectives to analysis of Paul's leadership. This is
a book of great balance using a biblically informed view of secular leadership theory along with a theoretically informed view of biblical leadership.

Eastman, Dick
1985   THE HOUR THAT CHANGES THE WORLD. Grand Rap-
          ids, Michigan: Baker.
Comments: Used as scan example.

Gerber, Virgil
1980   DISCIPLING THROUGH THEOLOGICAL EDUCATION BY
          EXTENSION. Chicago: Moody Press.
Comments: Referred to as worthy of ransack reading because of its
compilation of essay-like materials of several authors. The book does
not warrant evaluation reading.

Greenleaf, Robert K.
1977   SERVANT LEADERSHIP. New York: Paulist Press.
Comments: Era—Beginning of complexity era. Why Significant:
A book dealing with philosophical implications for leadership. Particularly calling for leadership in institutions to see institutions in terms
of a corporate servanthood toward society in general. Has Christian
presuppositional framework but written from secular standpoint.
A challenging book forcing us as leaders of organizations to examine
our reason for being and our responsibility beyond the bottom line.

Havelock, Ronald G.
1973   THE CHANGE AGENTS GUIDE TO INNOVATION IN EDU-
          CATION. Englewood Cliffs, N.J.: Educational Tech-
          nology Publications.

Comments: Uses the concept of a bridging strategy as a major means for designing planned change. The model was synthesized from change situations in the educational field but has much broader application than just educational change.

Hendricks, Howard

    1987   TEACHING TO CHANGE LIVES. Portland, Oregon: Multnomah Press.

Comments: Used as closed ransack example.

Hershey, P., & Blanchard, K. H.

    1977   MANAGEMENT OF ORGANIZATIONAL BEHAVIOR. Englewood Cliffs, N.J.: Prentice-Hall.

Comments: Era—Written during height of the Contingency Era. Why Significant—Hershey and Blanchard develop a model which takes into account many of the leadership variables. Their model does not hold to a "one-style" or "best-fit" approach as do other contingency models. It is a complex model which I feel best agrees with my own thinking. It is a book which is theoretically based yet communicates practically to one who wants to understand this model and thoroughly and use it and use it in a life situation. In short, it teaches that a leader must be flexible in his/her approach to styles and followers. As subordinates maturity increases, leader behavior should be characterized by a decreasing emphasis on consideration. As maturity continues to increase, there should be an eventual decrease in consideration. Maturity is defined in terms of subordinates' experience, achievement motivation, and willingness and ability to accept responsibility. It suggests that the power base that a leader uses should vary with situation and follower maturity.

Hodgkinson, Christopher

    1983   THE PHILOSOPHY OF LEADERSHIP. New York: St. Martin's Press.

Comments: Era—Written in the beginning of the Complexity Era. Why Significant—It is a prophetical call to reintroduce a philosophical stream back into the leadership elements.

Hollander, E. P.

1978   LEADERSHIP DYNAMICS: A PRACTICAL GUIDE TO EFFEC-
TIVE RELATIONSHIPS. New York: Free Press.

Comments: Transactional theory, utilized by Hollander, has a highregard
for followers.

Hunt, J. G., & Larson, L. L.

1977   LEADERSHIP: THE CUTTING EDGE. Carbondale: Southern Illinois University Press.

Comments: Era—Toward the end of the Contingency Era. Why Significant—Contains a good appraisal of Fiedler's theory, House's Path
Goal, gives a number of the questionnaires and scales that have been
used in research measurements including: LBDQ, LPC, U. of Michi-
gan 4-Factor scale. This issue has several articles which analyze
research methodology and problems with research methodology.
Greene's article, "Disenchantment with Leadership Research: Some
Causes, Recommendations, and Alternative Directions,"; Danserau and
Dumas' article, "Pratfalls and Pitfalls in Drawing Inferences about
Leader Behavior in Organizations,"; Melcher's article, "Leadership
Models and Research Approaches,"; and Butterfield and Bartol's, "Evalu-
ators of Leader Behavior: A Missing Element in Leadership Theory,"
are all worth study. This is the volume which also carried House's
outstanding article, "A 1976 Theory of Charismatic Leadership."

Kraft, Charles

1978   CHRISTIANITY IN CULTURE. New York: Orbis Books.

Comments: Referred to as a book worthy of study level reading. This
is a basal book in ethnotheology.

McGavran, Donald

1981   UNDERSTANDING CHURCH GROWTH. Revised Edition.
Grand Rapids: Eerdmans.

Comments: Referred to as a book worthy of study level reading. It is a
basal book in the field of church growth.

Mintzberg, Henry

> 1983   STRUCTURE IN FIVES - DESIGNING EFFECTIVE ORGANI-
> ZATIONS. Englewood Cliffs, N.J.: Prentice-Hall.

Comments: A comparative analysis of organizations in terms of structure. Mintzberg defines 5 major kinds of organizational configurations using 5 structural elements. Each configuration has a different profile (arrangement of the five structural elements).

Stanley, Paul and Bobby Clinton

> 1992   CONNECTING—FINDING THE MENTORING RELATION-
> SHIPS YOU NEED TO SUCCEED IN LIFE. Colorado Springs:
> Navpress.

Comments: This is a popular treatment of mentoring to help get people started into mentoring relationships.

Stogdill, Ralph Melvin

> 1948   PERSONAL FACTORS ASSOCIATED WITH LEADERSHIP: A SUR-
> VEY OF THE LITERATURE. In JOURNAL OF PSYCHOLOGY
>
> 1948   25, 35-71. Also occurs as Ch. 4 "Leadership Traits":
> 1904-1947 in Stogdill's, HANDBOOK OF LEADERSHIP:
> A SURVEY OF THEORY AND RESEARCH, (revised and ex-
> panded edition by Bernard M. Bass).

Comments: This is the watershed work that determined most of trait research. Its findings pointed leadership research toward importance of situation as a leadership variable. Researchers following this lead concentrated on leadership behavior for the next 20 years.

Wrong, Dennis H.

> 1980   POWER - ITS FORMS, BASES AND USES. New York:
> Harper & Row.
>
> Comment: This is a major book on power. It deals with
> power in terms of a fundamental definition,
> power bases, and power forms.

Yukl, Gary A.

    1981   LEADERSHIP IN ORGANIZATIONS. Englewood Cliffs, N.J.: Prentice-Hall.

Comments: Era—Beginning of Complexity Era. Why Significant—Primary focus of the book is managerial leadership, as opposed to parliamentary leadership, leadership of social movements, or informal leadership in peer groups. Leadership effectiveness is of special interest. Mixes theory and practice. Has excellent incisive (rather than comprehensive) bibliography. It is a foundational book which deals with an overview of what has been done in leadership as well as breaks new ground. The desperate person and topic indices are helpful.

Sample Outline Sheets

These sample outline sheets are for you to use as you begin to put into practice the tools detailed in this book. You can use the sample outline forms in this book or you can cut out on the dotted line and enlarge on a copier to put together your results from the various forms and types of readings as a resource for your continued growth and effectiveness in ministry.

SCAN READING

RANSACK READING

BROWSE READING

PRE-READING

IN-DEPTH READING/EVALUATION READING

OUTLINE SHEET FOR SCAN READING

Name of Person Doing Scan Reading: _____

Name of Book: _____

Time Involved: _____

6 SCAN RESULTS

1. Author:

2. Author's Perspective:

3. Organization of Book:

4. What the Author Intends to Accomplish:

5. Further Assessment Reading:

6. Further Evaluative Reading:

OUTLINE SHEET FOR SCAN READING

Name of Person Doing Scan Reading: _____

Name of Book: _____

Time Involved: _____

6 SCAN RESULTS

1. Author:

2. Author's Perspective:

3. Organization of Book:

4. What the Author Intends to Accomplish:

5. Further Assessment Reading:

6. Further Evaluative Reading:

OUTLINE SHEET FOR SCAN READING

Name of Person Doing Scan Reading: _____

Name of Book: _____

Time Involved: _____

6 SCAN RESULTS

1. Author:

2. Author's Perspective:

3. Organization of Book:

4. What the Author Intends to Accomplish:

5. Further Assessment Reading:

6. Further Evaluative Reading:

OUTLINE SHEET FOR SCAN READING

Name of Person Doing Scan Reading: _____

Name of Book: _____

Time Involved: _____

6 SCAN RESULTS

1. Author:

2. Author's Perspective:

3. Organization of Book:

4. What the Author Intends to Accomplish:

5. Further Assessment Reading:

6. Further Evaluative Reading:

OUTLINE SHEET FOR SCAN READING

Name of Person Doing Scan Reading: _____

Name of Book: _____

Time Involved: _____

6 SCAN RESULTS

1. Author:

2. Author's Perspective:

3. Organization of Book:

4. What the Author Intends to Accomplish:

5. Further Assessment Reading:

6. Further Evaluative Reading:

OUTLINE SHEET FOR SCAN READING

Name of Person Doing Scan Reading: _____

Name of Book: _____

Time Involved: _____

6 SCAN RESULTS

1. Author:

2. Author's Perspective:

3. Organization of Book:

4. What the Author Intends to Accomplish:

5. Further Assessment Reading:

6. Further Evaluative Reading:

OUTLINE SHEET FOR RANSACK READING

Name of Person Doing Ransack Reading: _____

Name of Book: _____

Time Involved: _____

___ Closed Ransacking - specific idea being ransacked:

___ Open Ransacking - general topic being ransacked:

6 Possible Ransack Results

1. New ideas or other helpful information on the pre-selected idea or topic:

2. Contrasting or differing idea on pre-selected idea or topic:

3. Nothing New of Note On Pre-Selected Topic or Idea
   Check here ___

4. Saw something of interest on Other than selected Idea or Topic

5. Nothing New Can Be Gained For This Book
   Check here ___

6. Decision For Further Reading
   ___ should read at browse level:
   ___ should read at pre-read level
   ___ should read at in-depth read level
   ___ should read at study level
   ___ no further reading needed

OUTLINE SHEET FOR RANSACK READING

Name of Person Doing Ransack Reading: _____

Name of Book: _____

Time Involved: _____

___ Closed Ransacking - specific idea being ransacked:

___ Open Ransacking - general topic being ransacked:

6 Possible Ransack Results

1. New ideas or other helpful information on the pre-selected idea or topic:

2. Contrasting or differing idea on pre-selected idea or topic:

3. Nothing New of Note On Pre-Selected Topic or Idea
   Check here ___

4. Saw something of interest on Other than selected Idea or Topic

5. Nothing New Can Be Gained For This Book
   Check here ___

6. Decision For Further Reading
   ___ should read at browse level:
   ___ should read at pre-read level
   ___ should read at in-depth read level
   ___ should read at study level
   ___ no further reading needed

OUTLINE SHEET FOR RANSACK READING

Name of Person Doing Ransack Reading: _____

Name of Book: _____

Time Involved: _____

___ Closed Ransacking - specific idea being ransacked:

___ Open Ransacking - general topic being ransacked:

6 Possible Ransack Results

1. New ideas or other helpful information on the pre-selected idea or topic:

2. Contrasting or differing idea on pre-selected idea or topic:

3. Nothing New of Note On Pre-Selected Topic or Idea
   Check here ___

4. Saw something of interest on Other than selected Idea or Topic

5. Nothing New Can Be Gained For This Book
   Check here ___

6. Decision For Further Reading
   ___ should read at browse level:
   ___ should read at pre-read level
   ___ should read at in-depth read level
   ___ should read at study level
   ___ no further reading needed

OUTLINE SHEET FOR RANSACK READING

Name of Person Doing Ransack Reading: _____

Name of Book: _____

Time Involved: _____

___ Closed Ransacking - specific idea being ransacked:

___ Open Ransacking - general topic being ransacked:

6 Possible Ransack Results

1. New ideas or other helpful information on the pre-selected idea or topic:

2. Contrasting or differing idea on pre-selected idea or topic:

3. Nothing New of Note On Pre-Selected Topic or Idea
   Check here ___

4. Saw something of interest on Other than selected Idea or Topic

5. Nothing New Can Be Gained For This Book
   Check here ___

6. Decision For Further Reading
   ___ should read at browse level:
   ___ should read at pre-read level
   ___ should read at in-depth read level
   ___ should read at study level
   ___ no further reading needed

OUTLINE SHEET FOR RANSACK READING

Name of Person Doing Ransack Reading: _____

Name of Book: _____

Time Involved: _____

___ Closed Ransacking - specific idea being ransacked:

___ Open Ransacking - general topic being ransacked:

6 Possible Ransack Results

1. New ideas or other helpful information on the pre-selected idea or topic:

2. Contrasting or differing idea on pre-selected idea or topic:

3. Nothing New of Note On Pre-Selected Topic or Idea
   Check here ___

4. Saw something of interest on Other than selected Idea or Topic

5. Nothing New Can Be Gained For This Book
   Check here ___

6. Decision For Further Reading
   ___ should read at browse level:
   ___ should read at pre-read level
   ___ should read at in-depth read level
   ___ should read at study level
   ___ no further reading needed

OUTLINE SHEET FOR RANSACK READING

Name of Person Doing Ransack Reading: _____

Name of Book: _____

Time Involved: _____

___ Closed Ransacking - specific idea being ransacked:

___ Open Ransacking - general topic being ransacked:

6 Possible Ransack Results

1. New ideas or other helpful information on the pre-selected idea or topic:

2. Contrasting or differing idea on pre-selected idea or topic:

3. Nothing New of Note On Pre-Selected Topic or Idea
   Check here ___

4. Saw something of interest on Other than selected Idea or Topic

5. Nothing New Can Be Gained For This Book
   Check here ___

6. Decision For Further Reading
   ___ should read at browse level:
   ___ should read at pre-read level
   ___ should read at in-depth read level
   ___ should read at study level
   ___ no further reading needed

OUTLINE SHEET FOR BROWSE READING

Name of Person Doing Browse Reading: _____

Name of Book: _____

Time Involved: _____

Unit Being Browsed:

___ 1. paragraphs: identify larger unit
___ 2. chapter sections (a consecutive group of paragraphs relating to a major idea of a chapter): identify extent of chapter section.
___ 3. whole chapters: identify which ones:
___ 4. parts of a section of a book (several chapters developing some single aspect of a major idea of a section of a book): Identify extent of the parts of the section:
___ 5. sections of a book (entire groups of chapters developing a major idea of the thesis of the book). Identify extent of the section:
___ 6. the whole book.

1. Note any observations of ideas, relevant insights, illustrations, biblical exegesis, quotes or other information useful to you. Where important, you may wish to identify the unit being browsed along with the relevant information.

2. Decision For Further Reading: A. The book should be read for thematic intent at the following evaluation read level:
___ (1) pre-read level
___ (2) in-depth read level
___ (3) study level b.
___ No further reading needed

OUTLINE SHEET FOR BROWSE READING

Name of Person Doing Browse Reading: _____

Name of Book: _____

Time Involved: _____

Unit Being Browsed:
- ___ 1. paragraphs: identify larger unit
- ___ 2. chapter sections (a consecutive group of paragraphs relating to a major idea of a chapter): identify extent of chapter section.
- ___ 3. whole chapters: identify which ones:
- ___ 4. parts of a section of a book (several chapters developing some single aspect of a major idea of a section of a book): Identify extent of the parts of the section:
- ___ 5. sections of a book (entire groups of chapters developing a major idea of the thesis of the book). Identify extent of the section:
- ___ 6. the whole book.

1. Note any observations of ideas, relevant insights, illustrations, biblical exegesis, quotes or other information useful to you. Where important, you may wish to identify the unit being browsed along with the relevant information.

2. Decision For Further Reading: A. The book should be read for thematic intent at the following evaluation read level:
- ___ (1) pre-read level
- ___ (2) in-depth read level
- ___ (3) study level b.
- ___ No further reading needed

OUTLINE SHEET FOR BROWSE READING

Name of Person Doing Browse Reading: _____

Name of Book: _____

Time Involved: _____

Unit Being Browsed:
___ 1. paragraphs: identify larger unit
___ 2. chapter sections (a consecutive group of paragraphs relating to a major idea of a chapter): identify extent of chapter section.
___ 3. whole chapters: identify which ones:
___ 4. parts of a section of a book (several chapters developing some single aspect of a major idea of a section of a book): Identify extent of the parts of the section:
___ 5. sections of a book (entire groups of chapters developing a major idea of the thesis of the book). Identify extent of the section:
___ 6. the whole book.

1. Note any observations of ideas, relevant insights, illustrations, biblical exegesis, quotes or other information useful to you. Where important, you may wish to identify the unit being browsed along with the relevant information.

2. Decision For Further Reading: A. The book should be read for thematic intent at the following evaluation read level:
___ (1) pre-read level
___ (2) in-depth read level
___ (3) study level b.
___ No further reading needed

OUTLINE SHEET FOR BROWSE READING

Name of Person Doing Browse Reading: _____

Name of Book: _____

Time Involved: _____

Unit Being Browsed:
___ 1. paragraphs: identify larger unit
___ 2. chapter sections (a consecutive group of paragraphs relating to a major idea of a chapter): identify extent of chapter section.
___ 3. whole chapters: identify which ones:
___ 4. parts of a section of a book (several chapters developing some single aspect of a major idea of a section of a book): Identify extent of the parts of the section:
___ 5. sections of a book (entire groups of chapters developing a major idea of the thesis of the book). Identify extent of the section:
___ 6. the whole book.

1. Note any observations of ideas, relevant insights, illustrations, biblical exegesis, quotes or other information useful to you. Where important, you may wish to identify the unit being browsed along with the relevant information.

2. Decision For Further Reading: A. The book should be read for thematic intent at the following evaluation read level:
___ (1) pre-read level
___ (2) in-depth read level
___ (3) study level b.
___ No further reading needed

OUTLINE SHEET FOR BROWSE READING

Name of Person Doing Browse Reading: _____

Name of Book: _____

Time Involved: _____

Unit Being Browsed:

___ 1. paragraphs: identify larger unit
___ 2. chapter sections (a consecutive group of paragraphs relating to a major idea of a chapter): identify extent of chapter section.
___ 3. whole chapters: identify which ones:
___ 4. parts of a section of a book (several chapters developing some single aspect of a major idea of a section of a book): Identify extent of the parts of the section:
___ 5. sections of a book (entire groups of chapters developing a major idea of the thesis of the book). Identify extent of the section:
___ 6. the whole book.

1. Note any observations of ideas, relevant insights, illustrations, biblical exegesis, quotes or other information useful to you. Where important, you may wish to identify the unit being browsed along with the relevant information.

2. Decision For Further Reading: A. The book should be read for thematic intent at the following evaluation read level:
___ (1) pre-read level
___ (2) in-depth read level
___ (3) study level b.
___ No further reading needed

OUTLINE SHEET FOR BROWSE READING

Name of Person Doing Browse Reading: _____

Name of Book: _____

Time Involved: _____

Unit Being Browsed:

___ 1. paragraphs: identify larger unit
___ 2. chapter sections (a consecutive group of paragraphs relating to a major idea of a chapter): identify extent of chapter section.
___ 3. whole chapters: identify which ones:
___ 4. parts of a section of a book (several chapters developing some single aspect of a major idea of a section of a book): Identify extent of the parts of the section:
___ 5. sections of a book (entire groups of chapters developing a major idea of the thesis of the book). Identify extent of the section:
___ 6. the whole book.

1. Note any observations of ideas, relevant insights, illustrations, biblical exegesis, quotes or other information useful to you. Where important, you may wish to identify the unit being browsed along with the relevant information.

2. Decision For Further Reading: A. The book should be read for thematic intent at the following evaluation read level:
___ (1) pre-read level
___ (2) in-depth read level
___ (3) study level b.
___ No further reading needed

OUTLINE SHEET FOR PRE-READING A BOOK

Name of Person Doing Pre Read: _____ **Date:** _____

Title of Book: _____

Author: _____

Time Involved: _____

1. Give here your statement describing the kind of book you pre-read. (See Step 1, page 38 for details of how to do this.)

2. Give here a statement describing the author's intent and methodology for carrying out that intent. (See Step 3, page 38 which is the primary help, and Steps 2 and 5 which sometimes help, page 38.)

3. Give here a single statement which clearly identifies the main subject of the book and weaves that subject to the major ideas developed about the subject. (Steps 1-5 all help do this.) Be sure that your major subject is clearly identified and that each major idea is clearly seen in its relationship to the major subject.

4. Give here your series of statements indicating how the author uses the structure of the book to develop his/her thesis statement identified in Step 3 above. (Step 4 helps on this, page 38.) Use the back of the sheet if more room is necessary.

5. Evaluate the miscellaneous helps in the book (i.e. various reference helps, such as indices, bibliography, footnotes, glossary, appendices, etc.).

OUTLINE SHEET FOR PRE-READING A BOOK

Name of Person Doing Pre Read: _____ **Date:** _____

Title of Book: _____

Author: _____

Time Involved: _____

1. Give here your statement describing the kind of book you pre-read. (See Step 1, page 38 for details of how to do this.)

2. Give here a statement describing the author's intent and methodology for carrying out that intent. (See Step 3, page 38 which is the primary help, and Steps 2 and 5 which sometimes help, page 38.)

3. Give here a single statement which clearly identifies the main subject of the book and weaves that subject to the major ideas developed about the subject. (Steps 1-5 all help do this.) Be sure that your major subject is clearly identified and that each major idea is clearly seen in its relationship to the major subject.

4. Give here your series of statements indicating how the author uses the structure of the book to develop his/her thesis statement identified in Step 3 above. (Step 4 helps on this, page 38.) Use the back of the sheet if more room is necessary.

5. Evaluate the miscellaneous helps in the book (i.e. various reference helps, such as indices, bibliography, footnotes, glossary, appendices, etc.).

OUTLINE SHEET FOR PRE-READING A BOOK

Name of Person Doing Pre Read: _____ **Date:** _____

Title of Book: _____

Author: _____

Time Involved: _____

1. Give here your statement describing the kind of book you pre-read. (See Step 1, page 38 for details of how to do this.)

2. Give here a statement describing the author's intent and methodology for carrying out that intent. (See Step 3, page 38 which is the primary help, and Steps 2 and 5 which sometimes help, page 38.)

3. Give here a single statement which clearly identifies the main subject of the book and weaves that subject to the major ideas developed about the subject. (Steps 1-5 all help do this.) Be sure that your major subject is clearly identified and that each major idea is clearly seen in its relationship to the major subject.

4. Give here your series of statements indicating how the author uses the structure of the book to develop his/her thesis statement identified in Step 3 above. (Step 4 helps on this, page 38.) Use the back of the sheet if more room is necessary.

5. Evaluate the miscellaneous helps in the book (i.e. various reference helps, such as indices, bibliography, footnotes, glossary, appendices, etc.).

OUTLINE SHEET FOR PRE-READING A BOOK

Name of Person Doing Pre Read: _____ **Date:** _____

Title of Book: _____

Author: _____

Time Involved: _____

1. Give here your statement describing the kind of book you pre-read. (See Step 1, page 38 for details of how to do this.)

2. Give here a statement describing the author's intent and methodology for carrying out that intent. (See Step 3, page 38 which is the primary help, and Steps 2 and 5 which sometimes help, page 38.)

3. Give here a single statement which clearly identifies the main subject of the book and weaves that subject to the major ideas developed about the subject. (Steps 1-5 all help do this.) Be sure that your major subject is clearly identified and that each major idea is clearly seen in its relationship to the major subject.

4. Give here your series of statements indicating how the author uses the structure of the book to develop his/her thesis statement identified in Step 3 above. (Step 4 helps on this, page 38.) Use the back of the sheet if more room is necessary.

5. Evaluate the miscellaneous helps in the book (i.e. various reference helps, such as indices, bibliography, footnotes, glossary, appendices, etc.).

OUTLINE SHEET FOR PRE-READING A BOOK

Name of Person Doing Pre Read: _____ **Date:** _____

Title of Book: _____

Author: _____

Time Involved: _____

1. Give here your statement describing the kind of book you pre-read. (See Step 1, page 38 for details of how to do this.)

2. Give here a statement describing the author's intent and methodology for carrying out that intent. (See Step 3, page 38 which is the primary help, and Steps 2 and 5 which sometimes help, page 38.)

3. Give here a single statement which clearly identifies the main subject of the book and weaves that subject to the major ideas developed about the subject. (Steps 1-5 all help do this.) Be sure that your major subject is clearly identified and that each major idea is clearly seen in its relationship to the major subject.

4. Give here your series of statements indicating how the author uses the structure of the book to develop his/her thesis statement identified in Step 3 above. (Step 4 helps on this, page 38.) Use the back of the sheet if more room is necessary.

5. Evaluate the miscellaneous helps in the book (i.e. various reference helps, such as indices, bibliography, footnotes, glossary, appendices, etc.).

OUTLINE SHEET FOR PRE-READING A BOOK

Name of Person Doing Pre Read: _____ **Date:** _____

Title of Book: _____

Author: _____

Time Involved: _____

1. Give here your statement describing the kind of book you pre-read. (See Step 1, page 38 for details of how to do this.)

2. Give here a statement describing the author's intent and methodology for carrying out that intent. (See Step 3, page 38 which is the primary help, and Steps 2 and 5 which sometimes help, page 38.)

3. Give here a single statement which clearly identifies the main subject of the book and weaves that subject to the major ideas developed about the subject. (Steps 1-5 all help do this.) Be sure that your major subject is clearly identified and that each major idea is clearly seen in its relationship to the major subject.

4. Give here your series of statements indicating how the author uses the structure of the book to develop his/her thesis statement identified in Step 3 above. (Step 4 helps on this, page 38.) Use the back of the sheet if more room is necessary.

5. Evaluate the miscellaneous helps in the book (i.e. various reference helps, such as indices, bibliography, footnotes, glossary, appendices, etc.).

OUTLINE SHEET FOR AN
IN-DEPTH READING OF A BOOK

Person Doing In-Depth Read: _____ **Date:** _____

Title of Book: _____

Author: _____

Time Involved: _____

1. Give the results of your pre-reading the above book for your statement of the author's thesis (a single statement which clearly identifies the main subject of the book and weaves that subject to the major idea developed about the subject. Be sure that your major subject is clearly identified and that each major idea is clearly seen in its relationship to the major subject. Use back of sheet if more room is needed for answer).

2. Give your evaluation statements concerning the following items. (If an evaluation statement does not apply - say so.) (Use the back of this sheet to continue your answers to the following questions when necessary.)

a. Examples where the author is uninformed:

b. Examples where the author is misinformed:

c. Examples where the author is illogical:

d. Examples where the author is incomplete in terms of purpose:

e. Strengths in the book:

f. Relevance of the book:

OUTLINE SHEET FOR AN
IN-DEPTH READING OF A BOOK

Person Doing In-Depth Read: _____ **Date:** _____

Title of Book: _____

Author: _____

Time Involved: _____

1. Give the results of your pre-reading the above book for your statement of the author's thesis (a single statement which clearly identifies the main subject of the book and weaves that subject to the major idea developed about the subject. Be sure that your major subject is clearly identified and that each major idea is clearly seen in its relationship to the major subject. Use back of sheet if more room is needed for answer).

2. Give your evaluation statements concerning the following items. (If an evaluation statement does not apply - say so.) (Use the back of this sheet to continue your answers to the following questions when necessary.)

a. Examples where the author is uninformed:

b. Examples where the author is misinformed:

c. Examples where the author is illogical:

d. Examples where the author is incomplete in terms of purpose:

e. Strengths in the book:

f. Relevance of the book:

OUTLINE SHEET FOR AN
IN-DEPTH READING OF A BOOK

Person Doing In-Depth Read: _____ **Date:** _____

Title of Book: _____

Author: _____

Time Involved: _____

1. Give the results of your pre-reading the above book for your statement of the author's thesis (a single statement which clearly identifies the main subject of the book and weaves that subject to the major idea developed about the subject. Be sure that your major subject is clearly identified and that each major idea is clearly seen in its relationship to the major subject. Use back of sheet if more room is needed for answer).

2. Give your evaluation statements concerning the following items. (If an evaluation statement does not apply - say so.) (Use the back of this sheet to continue your answers to the following questions when necessary.)

a. Examples where the author is uninformed:

b. Examples where the author is misinformed:

c. Examples where the author is illogical:

d. Examples where the author is incomplete in terms of purpose:

e. Strengths in the book:

f. Relevance of the book:

OUTLINE SHEET FOR AN
IN-DEPTH READING OF A BOOK

Person Doing In-Depth Read: _____ **Date:** _____

Title of Book: _____

Author: _____

Time Involved: _____

1. Give the results of your pre-reading the above book for your statement of the author's thesis (a single statement which clearly identifies the main subject of the book and weaves that subject to the major idea developed about the subject. Be sure that your major subject is clearly identified and that each major idea is clearly seen in its relationship to the major subject. Use back of sheet if more room is needed for answer).

2. Give your evaluation statements concerning the following items. (If an evaluation statement does not apply - say so.) (Use the back of this sheet to continue your answers to the following questions when necessary.)

a. Examples where the author is uninformed:

b. Examples where the author is misinformed:

c. Examples where the author is illogical:

d. Examples where the author is incomplete in terms of purpose:

e. Strengths in the book:

f. Relevance of the book:

OUTLINE SHEET FOR AN
IN-DEPTH READING OF A BOOK

Person Doing In-Depth Read: _____ **Date:** _____

Title of Book: _____

Author: _____

Time Involved: _____

1. Give the results of your pre-reading the above book for your statement of
    the author's thesis (a single statement which clearly identifies the main
    subject of the book and weaves that subject to the major idea developed
    about the subject. Be sure that your major subject is clearly identified and
    that each major idea is clearly seen in its relationship to the major subject.
    Use back of sheet if more room is needed for answer).

2. Give your evaluation statements concerning the following items. (If
    an evaluation statement does not apply - say so.) (Use the back of
    this sheet to continue your answers to the following questions when
    necessary.)

a. Examples where the author is uninformed:

b. Examples where the author is misinformed:

c. Examples where the author is illogical:

d. Examples where the author is incomplete in terms of purpose:

e. Strengths in the book:

f. Relevance of the book:

OUTLINE SHEET FOR AN
IN-DEPTH READING OF A BOOK

Person Doing In-Depth Read: _____ **Date:** _____

Title of Book: _____

Author: _____

Time Involved: _____

1. Give the results of your pre-reading the above book for your statement of the author's thesis (a single statement which clearly identifies the main subject of the book and weaves that subject to the major idea developed about the subject. Be sure that your major subject is clearly identified and that each major idea is clearly seen in its relationship to the major subject. Use back of sheet if more room is needed for answer).

2. Give your evaluation statements concerning the following items. (If an evaluation statement does not apply - say so.) (Use the back of this sheet to continue your answers to the following questions when necessary.)

a. Examples where the author is uninformed:

b. Examples where the author is misinformed:

c. Examples where the author is illogical:

d. Examples where the author is incomplete in terms of purpose:

e. Strengths in the book:

f. Relevance of the book:

BARNABAS PUBLISHERS

BARNABAS PUBLISHER'S MINI CATALOG

Approaching the Bible With Leadership Eyes: An Authoratative Source for Leadership Findings — Dr. J. Robert Clinton

Barnabas: Encouraging Exhorter — Dr. J. Robert Clinton & Laura Raab

Boundary Processing: Looking at Critical Transitions Times in Leader's Lives — Dr. J. Robert Clinton

Connecting: The Mentoring Relationships You Need to Succeed in Life — Dr. J. Robert Clinton

The Emerging Leader — Dr. J. Robert Clinton

Fellowship With God — Dr. J. Robert Clinton

Finishing Well — Dr. J. Robert Clinton

Figures and Idioms (Interpreting the Scriptures: Figures and Idioms) — Dr. J. Robert Clinton

Focused Lives Lectures — Dr. J. Robert Clinton

Gender and Leadership — Dr. J. Robert Clinton

Having A Ministry That Lasts: By Becoming a Bible Centered Leader — Dr. J. Robert Clinton

Hebrew Poetry (Interpreting the Scriptures: Hebrew Poetry) — Dr. J. Robert Clinton

A Short **History of Leadership Theory** — Dr. J. Robert Clinton

Isolation: A Place of Transformation in the Life of a Leader — Shelley G. Trebesch

Joseph: Destined to Rule — Dr. J. Robert Clinton

The Joshua Portrait — Dr. J. Robert Clinton and Katherine Haubert

Leadership Emergence Theory: A Self Study Manual For Analyzing the Development of a Christian Leader — Dr. J. Robert Clinton

Leadership Perspectives: How To Study The Bible for Leadership Insights — Dr. J. Robert Clinton

Coming to Some Conclusions on **Leadership Styles** — Dr. J. Robert Clinton

Leadership Training Models — Dr. J. Robert Clinton

The Bible and **Leadership Values:** A Book by Book Analysis— Dr. J. Robert Clinton

The Life Cycle of a Leader: Looking at God's Shaping of A Leader Towards An Eph. 2:10 Life — Dr. J. Robert Clinton

Listen Up Leaders! — Dr. J. Robert Clinton

The Mantle of the Mentor — Dr. J. Robert Clinton

Mentoring Can Help—Five Leadership Crises You Will Face in the Pastorate For Which You Have Not Been Trained — Dr. J. Robert Clinton

Mentoring: Developing Leaders...Without Adding More Programs — Dr. J. Robert Clinton

The Mentor Handbook: Detailed Guidelines and Helps for Christian Mentors and Mentorees — Dr. J. Robert Clinton

Moses Desert Leadership—7 Macro Lessons

Parables—Puzzles With A Purpose (Interpreting the Scriptures: Puzzles With A Purpose) — Dr. J. Robert Clinton

Paradigm Shift: God's Way of Opening New Vistas To Leaders — Dr. J. Robert Clinton

A Personal Ministry Philosophy: One Key to Effective Leadership — Dr. J. Robert Clinton

Reading on the Run: Continuum Reading Concepts — Dr. J. Robert Clinton

Samuel: Last of the Judges & First of the Prophets–A Model For Transitional Times — Bill Bjoraker

Selecting and Developing Those Emerging Leaders — Dr. Richard W. Clinton

Social Base Processing: The Home Base Environment Out of Which A Leader Works — Dr. J. Robert Clinton

Starting Well: Building A Strong Foundation for a Life Time of Ministry — Dr. J. Robert Clinton

Strategic Concepts: That Clarify A Focused Life – A Self Study Guide — Dr. J. Robert Clinton

The Making of a Leader: Recognizing the Lessons & Stages of Leadership Development — Dr. J. Robert Clinton

Time Line —Small Paper (What it is & How to Construct it) — Dr. J. Robert Clinton

Time Line: Getting Perspective—By Using Your Time-Line, Large Paper — Dr. J. Robert Clinton

Ultimate Contribution — Dr. J. Robert Clinton

Unlocking Your Giftedness: What Leaders Need to Know to Develop Themselves & Others — Dr. J. Robert Clinton

A **Vanishing Breed:** Thoughts About A Bible Centered Leader & A Life Long Bible Mastery Paradigm — Dr. J. Robert Clinton

The Way To Look At Leadership (How To Look at Leadership) — Dr. J. Robert Clinton

Webster-Smith, Irene: An Irish Woman Who Impacted Japan (A Focused Life Study) — Dr. J. Robert Clinton

Word Studies (Interpreting the Scriptures: Word Studies) — Dr. J. Robert Clinton

(Book Titles are in Bold and Paper Titles are in Italics with Sub-Titles and Pre-Titles in Roman)

BARNABAS PUBLISHERS

Unique Leadership Material that will help you answer the question:
"What legacy will you as a leader leave behind?"

"The difference between leaders and followers is perspective.
The difference between leaders and effective leaders is better perspective."
Barnabas Publishers has the materials that will help you find that
better perspective and a closer relationship with God.

BARNABAS PUBLISHERS

Post Office Box 6006 • Altadena, CA 91003-6006
Fax Phone (626)-794-3098 • Phone (626)-584-5393

CPSIA information can be obtained at www.ICGtesting.com
Printed in the USA
BVOW01s0612011014

369029BV00001B/78/A